The Easy-to-Use Guide
That Helps You Identify and Understand
Your Unique God-Given Spiritual Gifts

DISCOVER YOUR SPIRITUAL GIFTS

C. Peter Wagner

Regal

For more information and
special offers from Regal Books, email us at
subscribe@regalbooks.com

Published by Regal Books
From Gospel Light
Ventura, California, U.S.A.
Printed in the U.S.A.

Library of Congress Cataloging-in-Publication Data
Wagner, C. Peter.
  Discover your spiritual gifts / C. Peter Wagner.—Updated and expanded ed.
  p. cm.
  ISBN 978-0-8307-6231-6
  1. Gifts, Spiritual. I. Title.
  BT767.3.W33 2005
  234'.13—dc2   22004026309

Contents

A Fast Track
for Discovering Your Spiritual Gifts

You may have heard of spiritual gifts. Most Christian believers have, but not all. Possibly you are among those who have identified their spiritual gifts and have been using them on a regular basis. But a surprising number of believers who have heard of spiritual gifts are not sure what theirs may be. And there are even those who feel that, for some reason, they have been left out and do not have any of the gifts.

It is possible to be a member of a church, attend almost every Sunday and go for, let's say, a whole year without hearing anything about spiritual gifts. This is too bad. Why? Because in the first place, the teaching on spiritual gifts is so prominent in the New Testament. The apostle Paul says to the believers in the church in Corinth, "Now concerning spiritual gifts, brethren, I do not want you to be ignorant" (1 Cor. 12:1). All churches should make sure that they are moving in spiritual gifts. And in the second place, if you don't know about spiritual gifts, you may well miss out on God's best plan for your personal life.

This book will help you understand that if you are sure that you are a born-again member of the Body of Christ, you can be equally sure that you have one or more spiritual gifts. It will also set you on the road toward accurately identifying your gifts and then using them for their intended purposes. In fact, many readers will soon realize that they actually have been using one or more gifts without even recognizing that they are true spiritual gifts.

Once you start identifying your gifts, you will find that there are many excellent resources for helping you activate them. For example, my larger book on spiritual gifts, *Your Spiritual Gifts Can Help Your Church Grow*, has been circulating since the 1970s. Many are still buying it and reading it and applying the teachings to their own lives. However, there are those who never get around to reading it because they are not attracted to big books. I have realized that the fast-paced world in which we now live requires, for many, a smaller and more condensed manual like this one. Once you finish this, you may then wish to get the further details contained in *Your Spiritual Gifts Can Help Your Church Grow* or in many other excellent books on spiritual gifts.

Before going on, let me explain how the whole Body of Christ only recently woke up to the fact that God has given all of us one or more spiritual gifts.

REDISCOVERING
OUR SPIRITUAL GIFTS

A relatively new thing happened to the Church of Jesus Christ in America during the decade of the 1970s. The third Person of the Trinity began to come into His own, so to speak. Yes, the Holy Spirit has always been there. Creeds, hymns and liturgies have attested to the central place of the Holy Spirit in orthodox Christian faith. Systematic theologies throughout the centuries have included sections on pneumatology, thus affirming the Holy Spirit's place in Christian thought.

But rarely, if ever, in the history of the Church has such a widespread interest in moving beyond creeds and theologies to a personal experience of the Holy Spirit in everyday life swept over the people of God to the degree we now see in our churches. One of the most prominent facets of this new experience of the Holy Spirit is the rediscovery of spiritual gifts. Why do I say "rediscovery"?

FIXING THE DATE

It is fairly easy to fix the date when this new interest in spiritual gifts began. The production of literature itself is a reasonably accurate indicator. A decent seminary library may catalog something like 40 or 50 books on the subject of spiritual gifts. Probably more than 90 percent of them would have been written after 1970. Previous to 1970, seminary graduates characteristically left their institutions knowing little or nothing about spiritual gifts. The American Church was truly ignorant of spiritual gifts. Now almost every seminary or Bible college includes teaching on spiritual gifts as a part of its curriculum.

The Beginning

The roots of this new thing go back to 1900, the most widely accepted date for what is now known as the classical Pentecostal movement. During a watchnight service beginning on December 31, 1900, and ending on what is technically the first day of the twentieth century, Charles Parham of Topeka, Kansas, laid his hands on Agnes Ozman, she began speaking in tongues, and the movement had begun. A fascinating chain of events led to the famous Los Angeles Azusa Street Revival, which began in 1906 under the ministry of William Seymour. And with that, the Pentecostal movement gained high visibility and a momentum that has never slackened.

The original intent of Pentecostal leaders was to influence the major Christian denominations from within, reminiscent of the early intentions of such leaders as Martin Luther and John Wesley. But just as Lutheranism was found incompatible with the Catholic Church in the sixteenth century and just as Methodism was found incompatible with the Anglican Church in the eighteenth century, Pentecostalism found itself incompatible with the mainline American churches in the early twentieth century. Thus, as others had done before them, Pentecostal leaders reluctantly found it necessary to establish new denominations where they could develop a lifestyle directly under the influence of the Holy Spirit in an atmosphere of freedom and mutual support. Such denominations that we know today as Assemblies of God, Pentecostal Holiness, Church of God in Christ, Church of the Foursquare Gospel, Church of God (Cleveland, Tennessee) and many others were formed for that purpose.

The Second Phase

The second phase of this movement began after World War II when Pentecostal leaders set out to join the mainstream. The beginnings were slow. Some of the Pentecostal denominations began to gain social "respectability" by affiliating with organizations such as the National Association of Evangelicals. Consequently they began to neutralize the opinion that Pentecostalism was a kind of false cult to be placed alongside Jehovah's Witnesses, Mormons and spiritists.

In 1960, an Episcopal priest in Van Nuys, California, Dennis Bennett, shared with his congregation that he had experienced the Holy Spirit in the Pentecostal way, and what became known as the charismatic movement had its start. The charismatic movement took form first as renewal movements within major existing denominations, and then around 1970 the independent charismatic movement began with the emergence of freestanding charismatic churches separate from denominations. For the next 25 years, these independent charismatic churches were the fastest-growing group of churches in the United States.

The effect of all this soon began to be felt among Christians who were neither classical Pentecostals nor charismatics. Granted, many evangelical Christians still show little interest in experiencing the Pentecostal/charismatic "baptism in the Holy Spirit," accompanied by speaking in tongues. However, the broader distinguishing feature of these new movements is not just tongues, but rather the whole biblical dynamic of the operation of spiritual gifts in a new and exciting way. Through their discovery of how the gifts of the Spirit were intended to operate in the Body of Christ, the Holy Spirit is now being transformed from abstract doctrine to dynamic experience across the board.

We could not have said this before the 1970s.

WITNESSING THE DEMISE OF CESSATIONISM

Not everyone agrees, however. Some who remain cool on spiritual gifts, for example, argue that many of the gifts went out of use in the churches after the age of the apostles. An intellectual center of this belief is found at Dallas Theological Seminary, an interdenominational school that has looked with disfavor on the Pentecostal/charismatic movement of recent decades.

John Walvoord, former president of Dallas Seminary, feels that miracles, for example, have declined in the Church since the age of the apostles. His colleague Merrill Unger makes reference to Benjamin B. Warfield of Princeton Seminary who, back in 1918, wrote a book called *Miracles: Yesterday and Today, True and*

False. Other than the *Scofield Reference Bible,* it has been the most influential book written in America against the validity of the charismatic gifts today. Warfield argues that "these gifts were . . . distinctively the authentication of the Apostles. . . . Their function thus confined them to distinctively the Apostolic Church, and they necessarily passed away with it."[1]

The notion that the more spectacular spiritual gifts ceased with the apostolic age is now commonly known as cessationism. As I have detailed in my larger book *Your Spiritual Gifts Can Help Your Church Grow,* the charismatic gifts of the Holy Spirit have, in fact, been recognized by certain relatively small segments of the Church from time to time throughout Church history. But until quite recently, cessationism has been the prevailing Church doctrine. I was taught cessationism when I attended seminary back in the 1950s. Yet times are changing. Today, on a global scale, including in the United States, most Church leaders would agree that cessationism now belongs on some "endangered doctrines" list. The trend is definitely in the direction of expecting spiritual gifts to be as operative today as they were in the first century.

REALIZING THE MINISTRY OF ALL BELIEVERS

Spiritual gifts are given for ministry. The Bible says, "As each one has received a gift, minister it to one another, as good stewards of the manifold grace of God" (1 Peter 4:10). Since we have all received spiritual gifts, we are all expected to minister.

What I have just said makes such good sense and is so simple that it is difficult to understand why our classical theologians never saw it. You don't find the idea of all believers ministering with their spiritual gifts in our theological superstars such as Augustine or Martin Luther or John Calvin or John Wesley.

Martin Luther, for example, permanently changed Christendom when he rediscovered the priesthood of all believers back in the sixteenth century. Keep in mind that Luther was dealing with the teaching of the Catholic Church that ordinary believers, in order to get to God, had to go through a priest. His revolutionary teaching was that, according to the Bible, every believer had direct access to God, priest or no priest. Ever since then, the priesthood of all believers has been a fundamental tenet of our faith.

However, while Luther advocated the *priesthood* of all believers, he did not advocate the *ministry* of all believers through spiritual gifts. Neither did Calvin or Wesley. In fact, as late as the 1950s when I took my seminary training, only the priesthood of all believers, not the ministry of all believers, was being taught.

The Lutheranism of Martin Luther retained much of the clericalism of the Roman Catholic Church. "Clericalism" refers to the ministry of a local church being done by those who are ordained ministers. The members of the church, known as the laity, can assist the clergy by doing things such as singing in the choir or ushering or teaching children or cleaning the church or cooking for church suppers or serving on committees, but real church ministry is the job of the professionals.

Interestingly enough, when the Pentecostals began surfacing the concept of spiritual gifts in the early twentieth century, the form that their new churches took was about as clerical as the non-Pentecostal churches of the day. The emphasis was on the more spectacular gifts such as speaking in tongues, interpretation of tongues and prophecy, but the pastor was still regarded as the minister of the church. As I have said, it took until the 1970s for all of this to change.

As a matter of fact, I believe that 1972 can be considered the year that the concept of the *ministry* of all believers attained a permanent status in contemporary Christianity. Why 1972?

That was the year in which Ray Stedman's book *Body Life* was published, and it became an instant Christian best-seller. In his book, this highly respected non-Pentecostal pastor affirmed, in so many words, that spiritual gifts were OK. Although his list of the gifts turned out to be shorter than some others, because he also was a cessationist, Stedman showed clearly how spiritual gifts, the ministry of all believers and what he called Body life had brought new health, vitality and excitement to Peninsula Bible Church in Palo Alto, California.[2]

It remains a mystery to me why it took the Church until 1972 to understand the clear biblical teaching on spiritual gifts. Nevertheless, the ripple effects of the publication of *Body Life* have had a profound influence. Rare is the church today that will advocate that the professional pastor or staff should do all the ministry of the church. Although some churches have not been able to implement it as rapidly as others, most affirm, at least in theory, that laypeople should be empowered to discover their spiritual gifts and through them actually do the ministry of the church.

How this can become a reality in your life is what this book is all about.

MAKING IT PERSONAL

➔   Why does the subject of spiritual gifts interest you?

➔   How would you describe your relationship with the Holy Spirit?

➔   What concerns do you have about spiritual gifts?

Notes

1. Benjamin B. Warfield, *Miracles: Yesterday and Today, True and False* (Grand Rapids, MI: William B. Eerdmans Publishing Company, 1965), p. 6.
2. Ray C. Stedman, *Body Life* (Ventura, CA: Regal Books, 1972), n.p.

Being Everything
That God Wants You to Be

I was not brought up in a Christian home. Although it was a loving, functional family, the subject of religion was taboo in our household. We never went to church, we didn't pray, the word "Jesus" was only mentioned in expletives, and we were one of the 13 percent of American homes that did not own a copy of the Bible. Thinking back to my years growing up, I cannot recall knowing anyone who was a Christian.

So when I left home, I knew nothing about religion. In the course of events, I met a beautiful young woman whom I decided to marry. After a relatively brief courtship, I asked her if she would marry me. She said, "I can't." I said, "Why not?" She said, "Because I'm a born-again Christian, and I promised God that I would only marry a Christian." My response? "Well, what does it take to be a Christian? Can you show me how?" She told me that she could, so we knelt down in that farmhouse in upstate New York and I received Christ as my Lord and Savior. At this writing, Doris and I have celebrated our fifty-fourth wedding anniversary.

What does this have to do with spiritual gifts? At the time we were married, I was a university student. For all I knew, I was the only born-again Christian on the whole campus. I enrolled in a course on public speaking, and when my turn came to give a speech to the class, I decided to tell them about my conversion experience. Afterward, another student came up and told me that he also was a Christian and that a small group of Christians, as a part of InterVarsity Christian Fellowship, met together regularly on campus. I immediately joined them, and they started teaching me how to live the Christian life.

One of the things they taught me to do was to memorize Scripture. They told me to memorize Romans 12:1-2: "I beseech you therefore, brethren, by the mercies of God, that you present your bodies a living sacrifice, holy, acceptable to God, which is your reasonable service. And do not be conformed to this world, but be transformed by the renewing of your mind, that you may prove what is that good and acceptable and perfect will of God." I loved this verse because, as a new believer, I was so thankful to God for saving me that I wanted desperately to do His "good and acceptable and perfect will."

But when I thought about what Romans 12:1-2 said about doing God's will, I realized that I was in over my head. Present my body a living sacrifice? Don't be conformed to this world? Transformed by the renewing of the mind? As a new uninstructed believer, I had no idea what these rather abstract concepts could mean for me.

Later I discovered that my mistake had been to stop memorizing this passage with verse 2. If I had added the next four verses, the abstract would have become very concrete. Here is where spiritual gifts come into the picture.

This Scripture passage goes on to say that the key to coming to practical terms with the will of God for our lives involves, first of all, not thinking more highly of ourselves than we ought to think (see Rom. 12:3). In other words, there is no room for pride. All right, we must be humble.

But the other side of that same coin is to "think soberly" (v. 3) of ourselves. This obviously means that each of us needs a realistic self-evaluation as a starting point for doing the good and effective and perfect will of God. How do we go about this?

The first clue is to recognize that part of our personal spiritual constitution is a "measure of faith" (v. 3), which God has distributed to every Christian person. The implication is that each Christian will probably receive a different measure and, therefore, every believer is unique. But unique in what sense? Before Paul answers this question, he gives us the analogy he is preparing to use in order to help us understand spiritual gifts, namely, the analogy of the human body: "For as we have many members in one body, but all the members do not have the same function, so we, being many, are one body in Christ" (vv. 4-5).

WHAT IS THE
BODY OF CHRIST?

What, precisely, is the "Body of Christ" to which we have been introduced? This is a very important question because in every one of the three major biblical passages on spiritual gifts, namely, Romans 12, 1 Corinthians 12 and Ephesians 4, the gifts are directly compared to members of the human body. Because the Bible says that we Christians are all one Body in Christ, we understand that it is a group of believers. It is the Church. This is confirmed in Colossians 1:18: "[Jesus Christ] is the head of the body, the church."

But how did God decide to organize the Church, the Body of Christ?

On the one hand, God did not plan that the Body of Christ should be organized around the model of a dictatorship, in which just one person rules, benevolent as that person might be. Martin Luther reacted against that idea, and so should we. On the other hand, neither did God intend that the Church should be a democracy, in which every member rules. This latter point needs to be emphasized, especially here in America, where our civil culture prides itself so much on democracy and where this cultural value is frequently carried over into our churches as if democracy were a biblical principle, which it is not.

Instead of making the Body of Christ a dictatorship or a democracy, God has chosen to make it a living *organism,* Jesus being the head and each member functioning with one or more spiritual gifts. Understanding spiritual gifts, then, is the foundational key to understanding the organization of the Church.

The major biblical passages on spiritual gifts reinforce the above conclusion. It cannot be mere coincidence, as I have mentioned, that in all three of the explicit passages on spiritual gifts, Romans 12, 1 Corinthians 12 and Ephesians 4, the gifts are explained in the context of the Body. To be specific, Romans 12:4-5 reads, "For as we have many members in one body, but all the members do not have the same function, so we, being many, are one body in Christ, and individually members of one another." First Corinthians 12:18 reads, "God has set the members, each one of them, in the body just as He pleased." Ephesians 4:16 reads, "From whom [Christ] the whole body, joined and knit together by what every joint supplies, according to the effective working by which every part does its share, causes growth of the body for the edifying of itself in love." This means that God has not only designed the Body on the model of an organism, but He has also gone so far as to determine what the function of each of the individual members should be.

If each one of us knows what our particular function is in the Body, we are then able to "think soberly" of ourselves and to launch into doing the will of God. Simply put, do you want to do the good and effective and perfect will of God, as Romans 12:2 says? If so, an essential step, not an optional one, is to know for sure what spiritual gifts He has given you.

WHO HAS SPIRITUAL GIFTS?

Not everybody in the world has spiritual gifts. Unbelievers do not. But every Christian person who is committed to Jesus and truly a member of His Body has at least one gift and quite possibly more. The Bible says that every Christian has received a gift (see 1 Pet. 4:10) and that "the manifestation of the Spirit is given to each one for the profit of all" (1 Cor. 12:7). First Corinthians 12:18, as we have just seen, stresses that *every one* of the members is placed in the Body according to God's design. Possession of one or more spiritual gifts is part of God's plan for every Christian.

This comes as good news to the average believer. It is wonderful to be assured that God knows me, He loves me, and He considers me special enough to give me a personal gift so that I can serve Him. This is especially true in a society such as ours in America, where many school districts establish special programs for "gifted children." The implication of that is that ordinary citizens aren't gifted. Not so in the Body of Christ! God gifts us all!

WHAT ARE GIFT-MIXES?

Many Christians are multigifted. In fact, I would suspect that probably the majority of Christians, or perhaps even all, have what we could call a gift-mix, instead of a single gift.

Given the variety of spiritual gifts, the degrees of giftedness in each personal case and the multiple ministries through which each gift can be exercised, the combination of these qualities that each one of us has been given may be the most important factor in determining our spiritual personalities. Most of us are used to the idea that each individual has his or her own personality. For example, my wife, Doris, and I have three daughters, all born of the same parents and raised in the same household, but each one of them is unique. God's children are similar. All Christians are unique members of the Body of Christ, and their individual identity is determined to a significant degree by the gift-mix that God has given them.

The health of the Church and its subsequent growth depend on this fact. I realize that it comes as a surprise to some Christians, who may have been only marginally active in church for years, to find out that they are actually needed, wanted and gifted to do their part in their local church. But it is true. In order for you to be everything that God wants you to be, there is no substitute for finding your gift-mix and knowing for sure that you are equipped to do the "good and acceptable and perfect will of God" (Rom. 12:2).

WHAT IS THE RELATIONSHIP BETWEEN GOD'S GIFTS AND GOD'S CALL?

Christians often speak of their calling. We frequently say things like "God has *called* me to do such and such" or "I don't believe God is *calling* me to do such and such." At this point, it is helpful to recognize that a person's call and his or her spiritual gifts are closely associated.

When related to doing God's will, your *general* call should be seen as equivalent to your spiritual gift. No better framework exists within which to interpret your call than to know your specific gift-mix. God does not give you gifts that He does not *call* you to use, nor does He *call* you to do something for Him without equipping you with the necessary gift or gifts to do it.

Besides a *general* calling, however, you may also have a more *specific* calling. Some like to refer to this specific call as a person's ministry. Your ministry is the particular way or the particular setting in which God wishes you to exercise the gift or gifts that He has given you. For example, you can have the gift of teaching and be called specifically to use that gift among children; others may use the gift of teaching on the radio or in writing books or in the pulpit. You can have the missionary gift and be called to use that gift in Zambia; others may be called to Paraguay or to Sri Lanka or to a different ethnic group in their own American city. Within the general calling provided by each gift, then, are many more specific ways that God assigns such a gift to be ministered by different believers.

WHAT IS
A SPIRITUAL GIFT?

At this point, let's pause and define just what "spiritual gift" means. The working definition I like to use is as follows:

> *A spiritual gift is a special attribute given by the Holy Spirit to every member of the Body of Christ, according to God's grace, for use within the context of the Body.*

This is as tight a definition as I have been able to formulate and still retain what I consider to be the essential elements. Two of these elements, namely, "special attribute" and "to every member of the Body of Christ," have been sufficiently discussed. Three other important phrases remain.

According to God's Grace

"According to God's grace" is a phrase that moves us into the biblical words themselves. The common Greek word for spiritual gift is *charisma;* the plural is *charismata.* Our contemporary terms "charismatic movement" and "charismatics" are derived from this Greek word. But note something else. "Charisma" comes from the root word *charis,* which in Greek means "grace." A close relationship exists, then, between spiritual gifts and the grace of God.

By the Holy Spirit

Let's look at the phrase "given by the Holy Spirit." Unfortunately, there have been some people who have taught, mostly carrying over excesses in early Pentecostalism, that if you want a certain gift bad enough, you can have it if you agree to do the right things. There are even seminars that assure you that if you register and attend and follow instructions, you will leave with the gift. Think of the implications of this. It implies that your efforts, or your works, can get you a gift. If this is the case, it violates the principle of grace that we have just established. In other words, it takes the "charis" out of "charisma."

Here is the biblical truth, pure and simple: "But one and the same Spirit works all these things [spiritual gifts], distributing to each one individually as He wills" (1 Cor. 12:11). And "God has set the members, each one of them, in the body just as He pleased" (v. 18). You have your gifts, not because you chose them, but because God chose them for you.

Some will respond to this by quoting 1 Corinthians 12:31, "But earnestly desire the best gifts," followed up by 1 Corinthians 14:1, "Pursue love, and desire spiritual gifts." Doesn't this indicate that the desire we have for certain spiritual gifts has something to do with the ones we receive? Good question! Let me give two responses.

First, when I checked out 1 Corinthians 12 and 14 in the original Greek, I found that both of these admonitions to "desire" are directed collectively to the whole church at Corinth, not to individuals. The church there was overutilizing the gift of tongues and underutilizing the gift of prophecy. That is what Paul wanted to correct.

But my second response relates to you as an individual. Should you pray that God will give you a gift that you really want to have? Here is my answer: If you are a committed Christian, if you are living a holy life and if you are filled with the Holy Spirit, you can be assured that if God has chosen to give you a certain gift, He is also, more often than not, going to create in you the desire to receive that gift. Your desire is not from your carnal nature, but from the Holy Spirit. Then you should pray for it, keeping in mind that it is God, by His grace and not by your works, who has initiated the whole process.

For Use Within the Body

The final phrase of the definition, "for use within the context of the Body," reminds us that individual Christians disconnected from the Body are not as useful as they could be. Spiritual gifts are not designed for Lone Rangers. They are designed for members of the Body. Most of the things God does in the world today is done through believers who are working together in community and complementing each other with their gifts, not only in their local congregations, but also in the workplace.

The biblical Greek word for "Church" is *ekklesia*, which refers to the people of God. Sometimes the people of God are gathered and sometimes they are scattered. Most Christians are affiliated with local congregations that gather together one day a week. In our minds, the word "Church" has been strongly tied to these local congregations. However, most of the people of God spend the other six days of the week out there in the workplace. When they are in the workplace, are they still the Church? Yes, because they are still the ekklesia, the people of God. The terminology I like best for these two forms of the same Church is "nuclear Church," namely, the Church gathered together once a week; and "extended Church," the Church scattered the rest of the week.

In light of this, spiritual gifts are operative "within the context of the Body," as the definition says, wherever the people of God are found. Most of the information we currently have on the practical application of spiritual gifts relates to the nuclear Church. However, a movement sometimes called faith at work has recently gained widespread acceptance in Christian circles, and many leaders are actively analyzing just how the whole range of spiritual gifts operates within the extended Church. This comes as good news to believers who spend most of their lives in the workplace and who meet together in a local church building only one day a week. What they do in the workplace, like repairing automobiles or writing insurance policies or teaching school, is legitimate ministry just as much as singing on the worship team or leading a home group or serving on a church board.

This means that spiritual gifts are needed for ministry seven days a week.

ARE YOU READY TO DISCOVER, DEVELOP AND USE YOUR GIFT?

If putting your spiritual gifts into practice is a key to help you be all that God wants you to be, let's get practical. In light of the clear teaching of God's Word, I think it is safe to say that one of the primary spiritual exercises for any Christian person is to discover, develop and use his or her spiritual gift. Other spiritual exercises may be equally as important, such as worship, prayer, reading God's Word, feeding the hungry, the sacraments or what have you. But I do not know of anything *more* important than discovering, developing and using your spiritual gifts.

Notice that I put "discovering" before "developing." This is because spiritual gifts are *received*, not *achieved*. Let me repeat that God gives the gifts at His own discretion. First Corinthians 12:11 talks about the Spirit distributing gifts "to each one individually *as He wills*" (emphasis added). Later in verse 18 the text says that God sets the members in the Body *"just as He pleased"* (emphasis added). God has not entrusted any human being to give spiritual gifts. No pastor, no district superintendent, no seminary president, not even the Pope himself is qualified to distribute spiritual gifts.

WHAT ARE THE BENEFITS OF SPIRITUAL GIFTS?

What happens if you do decide to discover, develop and use your spiritual gift or gifts? Several things.

First of all, you will be a better Christian and will be better able to allow God to make your life count for Him. People who know their gifts have a handle on their spiritual job description, so to speak. They find their place in the church with more ease.

Christian people who know their spiritual gifts tend to develop healthy self-esteem. This does not mean they "think of [themselves] more highly than [they] ought to think" (Rom. 12:3). Instead, they learn that no matter what their gift is, they are important to God and to the Body. The ear learns not to say, "Because I am not an eye, I am not of the body" (1 Cor. 12:16). Crippling inferiority complexes drop by the wayside when people begin to "think soberly" of themselves (Rom. 12:3).

Some are inhibited by a misguided idea of humility. They refuse to name their spiritual gift on the grounds that this might be seen as arrogant or presumptuous on their part. This unfortunate mind-set only exhibits their failure to understand the biblical teaching on gifts. Others may have a less noble motive for not wanting to be associated with a gift—they might know that they have a spiritual gift, but they do not want to be held accountable for its use. In that case, appealing to humility can be used as a cover-up for disobedience.

Second, not only does knowing about spiritual gifts help individual Christians, but it also helps the Church as a whole. The Bible tells us that when spiritual gifts are in operation, the whole Body matures. It helps the Body to gain "the measure of the stature of the fullness of Christ" (Eph. 4:13).

The third and most important thing that knowing about spiritual gifts does is that it glorifies God. The apostle Peter advises believers to use their spiritual gifts and then adds the reason why: "That in all things God may be glorified through Jesus Christ, to whom belong the glory and the dominion forever and ever. Amen" (1 Pet. 4:11). What could be better than glorifying God? I agree with the *Westminster Shorter Catechism*, which affirms that glorifying God is "man's chief end."

If using spiritual gifts helps me glorify God, I want to use my gifts! I know that you do also. It helps all of us be everything that God wants us to be!

MAKING IT PERSONAL

➜   What are your beliefs about the giftedness of every Christian to serve God?

➜   What is your personal experience with spiritual gifts?

➜   What motivates you to discover, develop and use your spiritual gift-mix?

CHAPTER THREE

How Many Gifts
Are There?

If we, the Body of Christ, the Church, function best with each member using the spiritual gifts that he or she has been given, it becomes important to be able to identify the part that each plays. We are a team. Good baseball teams, for example, understand perfectly the differing roles of a first baseman or a pitcher or a center fielder or a catcher or a third-base coach.

The biblical analogy for understanding spiritual gifts is the human body. The parts of our human body all have names. God possibly chose the human body as the physical example of the Church because each human being, regardless of educational level, can accurately identify body parts. Everyone knows the position and function of a toe or an eyebrow or a lung or a hip or a tooth or whatever. We need to be just as familiar with the Body parts of the Church, characterized by the spiritual gifts that God has distributed.

So, how many spiritual gifts are there, and what are they for?

OUTLINING THE THREE KEY LISTS

The great majority of the spiritual gifts mentioned in the Bible are found in three key chapters: Romans 12, 1 Corinthians 12 and Ephesians 4. Mark these three locations in your Bible for future reference, because they are primary. Several secondary chapters also provide other important details; these include mainly 1 Corinthians 7, 1 Corinthians 13–14, Ephesians 3 and 1 Peter 4.

I will begin putting our master list of gifts together by using the three primary chapters. The words in parentheses will be variant translations found in several different English versions of the Bible.

Romans 12:6-8 mentions the following spiritual gifts:

1. Prophecy (preaching, inspired utterance)
2. Service (ministry)
3. Teaching
4. Exhortation (stimulating faith, encouraging)
5. Giving (contributing, generosity, sharing)
6. Leadership (authority, ruling)
7. Mercy (sympathy, comfort to the sorrowing, showing kindness)

First Corinthians 12:8-10 and 28 adds (without repeating those already listed from Romans):

8. Wisdom (wise advice, wise speech)
9. Knowledge (studying, speaking with knowledge)
10. Faith
11. Healing
12. Miracles (doing great deeds)
13. Discerning of spirits (discrimination in spiritual matters)
14. Tongues (speaking in languages never learned, ecstatic utterance)

15. Interpretation of tongues
16. Apostle
17. Helps
18. Administration (governments, getting others to work together)

Ephesians 4:11 adds
(again, without repeating any of the above):

19. Evangelist
20. Pastor (caring for God's people)

COMPLETING
THE MASTER LIST

The three primary chapters give us 20 separate gifts, but that is not all that there are.

One thing becomes immediately evident from looking at these three primary lists—none of the lists is complete in itself. Some gifts mentioned in Ephesians are mentioned in Romans, and some in Romans are mentioned in 1 Corinthians, and some in 1 Corinthians are mentioned in Ephesians. Apparently, none of them is intended to be a complete catalog of the gifts God gives. And we could surmise that if none of the three lists is complete in itself, probably the three lists together, or the 20 gifts, are not complete.

The Bible itself confirms that this is a correct assumption. At least five other gifts are mentioned in the New Testament as spiritual gifts:

21. Celibacy (continence) (1 Cor. 7:7)
22. Voluntary poverty (1 Cor. 13:3)
23. Martyrdom (1 Cor. 13:3)

24. Missionary (Eph. 3:6-8)
25. Hospitality (1 Pet. 4:9)

DETERMINING WHETHER ALL GIFTS ARE MENTIONED IN THE BIBLE

These 25 spiritual gifts turn out to be all those mentioned in the Bible as gifts. But this biblical list, as I have said, is apparently not intended to be exhaustive. Now this raises an interesting question. Could it be that there are some legitimate spiritual gifts, given by God to certain believers, that are not mentioned specifically as gifts in the Bible? Naturally, there are two possible answers to this question, and each of the answers has its supporting points. So if you feel that it is best to leave the list with 25, I would not quarrel with you. But my own personal conclusion is that some other real gifts are actually in use.

I have come to this conclusion after years of careful observation. I tend to think that there are three spiritual gifts that are not referred to as gifts in Scripture. The ministries that the three are designed to accomplish, however, are definitely biblical. If this were not the case, I would not consider them at all. But don't ask me for Bible verses that prove beyond the shadow of a doubt that they are actually spiritual gifts per se.

I was gratified when I read the works of several other scholars who agree that there may be legitimate spiritual gifts in the Church that are not mentioned as gifts in the Bible. A number of them bring up three gifts, which they suggest be added but which I have chosen *not* to add, namely, craftsmanship, preaching and writing. I must admit that I do not have really strong arguments against adding these, so I leave the question open.

For years, my material on spiritual gifts has included two other gifts, based on my empirical observation of Church life and ministry. These are the spiritual gifts of intercession and deliverance. That would bring my total up from 25 to 27.

However, as readers of some of my other books know, I have more recently transitioned from traditional Christianity to the New Apostolic Reformation. One of the big differences that was obvious from the outset is that worship in apostolic churches is radically different from worship in traditional churches. I have now observed something that was not on my radar screen when I did my previous books on spiritual gifts: There must be a spiritual gift of leading worship. This is more than possessing certain musical skills. It is more than functioning as a pastor or minister of music. It is a God-given ability to usher others into the very presence of God in an extraordinary way. So leading worship is now number 28 on my list of spiritual gifts.

While we're on the subject of leading worship, it is interesting to observe that the contemporary worship style, which originally emerged from the apostolic churches, has rapidly gained popularity in denominational churches across the board. This means that the gift of leading worship promises to be more and more in demand throughout the Body of Christ in the days to come, and it is now included in the Wagner-Modified Houts Questionnaire.

Here, then, is the conclusion of my list of 28 spiritual gifts:

26. Intercession
27. Deliverance (exorcism, casting out demons)
28. Leading worship (music)

DISTINGUISHING GIFTS FROM OFFICES

Some may observe the fact that the list of spiritual gifts in Ephesians 4 is slightly different from the other two because it refers to individuals who have *offices* rather than the underlying *gifts* as such. This is correct. Paul says, "And [Christ] Himself gave some to be apostles, some prophets, some evangelists, and some pastors and teachers" (Eph. 4:11). I find it helpful to see these as the foundational, or governmental, offices of the Church. The focus is thereby placed on gifted people who have been recognized in such official positions. Usually, such people have been ordained, or commissioned, with a public laying on of hands.

The first thing to notice is that each one of these offices is fundamentally determined by the spiritual gift that God has given to the individual. The gift of prophecy, not the office, is mentioned in both Romans 12:6 and 1 Corinthians 12:10. The gift of teaching is mentioned both in Romans 12:7 and 1 Corinthians 12:28. The gift of apostle is found in 1 Corinthians 12:28. There are no direct references to the gift of pastor or the gift of evangelist, but it would not be stretching the point to assume that a person can't have the office of pastor without the gift of pastor or the office of evangelist without the gift of evangelist.

This means that you can have a gift without an office, but you cannot have an office without a gift. You can have the gift of prophecy without being recognized as a prophet. You can have the gift of apostle without being awarded the office. I say "awarded" because the office is earned. Gifts, as we have seen, are given only by the grace of God. But offices are not given by grace; they are merited through works. In other words, God may have given me the gift of apostle, but if I do not display the fruit of this gift through my ministry in the Body, I will never move into the office.

The office is the official recognition on the part of the Body of Christ that a person has a certain spiritual gift, or a gift-mix, and that such a person is authorized to use that gift in public ministry. We are most accustomed to doing that with the gift of pastor and recognizing it through what we call ordination. Ordination does not give a person the gift of pastor—it assumes that God has already done that. Rather, ordination is an affirmation that responsible people have observed that the candidate has the gift and that it should be recognized and affirmed and supported by the rest of the Body.

RECOGNIZING THAT EVERY GIFT IS IN THE MINORITY

Since obviously not everyone is a pastor or a prophet or an apostle, this raises an important general principle relating to spiritual gifts: More members of the Body of Christ do not share any particular spiritual gift than those who do share it. Let's consider the gift of celibacy for a moment in order to establish this principle.

The reason that we have included celibacy on the list of spiritual gifts is that 1 Corinthians 7 labels it as such. In that chapter, Paul is establishing the fact that those who are single, as he was, can use more of their time and energy in directly serving the Lord than can married people. He realizes, however, that God created human beings with glands and hormones and passions, so the normal thing is for men and women to grow up, marry each other and have families. It is better for such people "to marry than to burn with passion" (v. 9), he says. Nevertheless, there are some, like Paul, to whom God has given the gift of celibacy. He attributes this to "each one [having] his own gift from God" (v. 7).

What, then, is the principle? It is obvious that most human beings, Christian or non-Christian, are destined by God to marry and have families. That means that those who have the gift of celibacy and who serve the Lord by remaining unmarried are clearly in the minority. But think about it. The same thing would be true of the other 27 gifts on the list. Every spiritual gift is in the minority.

This would be confirmed by going back to the analogy of the human body. Every part of our bodies is, in fact, a minority. We have only 2 hips, 1 nose, 2 ears, 36 teeth, 2 kidneys, 10 toes, 1 esophagus and so forth. More parts of your body are *not* a certain member than *are*, no argument. But this also would apply to the Body of Christ. That is why Paul would ask the rhetorical questions, "If the whole body were an eye, where would be the hearing? If the whole were hearing, where would be the smelling?" (1 Cor. 12:17). Many others will undoubtedly have the same spiritual gift that you have, but the majority will not. And we all need each other to make the whole Body work.

I believe that it is reasonable to conclude that something less than 50 percent of the Body should ordinarily be expected to have any particular gift. Furthermore, my hunch is that most of the percentages will come out far less than 50 percent. I have done some research on the gift of evangelist, for example, and found that the figure is probably around 5 percent. The gift of missionary appears to be less than 1 percent and the gift of intercession somewhere around 5 percent. Just like we don't need three eyes, we don't need more of gifts like these in order to accomplish God's purposes. God both assigns the gifts and determines the ratio of the gifts in the Body.

PAIRING UP:
HYPHENATED GIFTS

Some make a point that in Ephesians 4:11 the gifts most often listed as "pastors" and "teachers" should not be separate, but they should be combined as "pastor-teachers." They argue that the Greek construction could lead to the conclusion that pastor-teacher is really one gift, not two different gifts. This is one way of interpreting the verse, but it's not the only way.

In my opinion, there is a better explanation. I think that many of the gifts on the list very frequently pair up with each other and that it is most helpful to regard them as "hyphenated gifts" when an individual has both. For example, it is obvious that not every teacher is also a pastor and not every pastor is also a teacher. But a large number of people are pastor-teachers because they have been given both gifts.

There are several other common pairings of gifts. For example, there are intercession-prophecy, knowledge-teaching, deliverance-discerning of spirits, apostle-leadership and healing-miracles, just to name a few.

HONORING ALL VARIATIONS AND DEGREES OF GIFTS

Within almost every one of the 28 spiritual gifts will be found a wide range of variations and degrees. The cue for this might be seen in 1 Corinthians 12:4-6, where the Bible speaks of gifts (*charismaton*), ministries (*diakonion*) and activities (*energematon*). Ray Stedman defines "ministry" as "the sphere in which a gift is performed" and an "activity" (or working) as "the degree of power by which a gift is manifested or ministered on a specific occasion."[1]

A person who has the gift of evangelist, for example, might be a personal evangelist or a public evangelist—different ministries using the same gift. One who has the ministry of public evangelism might be an international celebrity who fills stadiums with 50,000 people and sees 3,000 conversions in a week. That would be the activity. Another public evangelist might be assigned to an activity mostly in churches that hold 500 people and might see

30 conversions in a week. In the final analysis, both may be found to be equally faithful in the exercise of their gift.

Variations and degrees, as the gifts themselves, are distributed at the discretion of God. Just as the master in the parable of the talents gave to one five talents, to another two and to yet another one (see Matt. 25:15), so God in His wisdom gives to each of us "a measure of faith" (Rom. 12:3). This is why, when gifts are in operation properly, Christians who have different degrees of the same gift have no cause for jealousy or envy. My left hand is not envious of my right hand because it may not be able to develop skills equal to my right hand. Rather, the two hands work together harmoniously for the benefit of my whole body. Similarly, God has given me a gift for writing, but in a relatively moderate degree. I am realistic enough to know that scores of others—Martin Marty or George Otis, Jr., or Jerry Jenkins or John Stott, just to name a few who come to mind—have such a high degree of the gift that I am not worthy to be mentioned in the same breath.

CLASSIFYING THE GIFTS

The gifts can be classified in many different ways. Bill Gothard, for example, divides them into "motivations," "ministries" and "manifestations."[2] Some Reformed theologians have separated "ordinary gifts" from "extraordinary gifts." I have seen gifts divided into "enabling gifts," "servicing gifts" and "tongues/interpretation." There could be others.

Some of the people who use these classifications have had excellent success in teaching Christians to discover, develop and use their spiritual gifts. I applaud whatever classification they use as long as it works. Obviously, none of these humanly designed classifications is divinely inspired.

In my own teaching, as I have said before, I prefer the open-ended approach. I do not find it particularly helpful to classify the gifts. The reason I have taken this route is not necessarily because I think it is any more biblical than the others but simply because I have found it to be the most helpful approach for my own particular teaching style. It works well for me, and it may work for you as well.

MAKING IT PERSONAL

 Which, if any, of the gifts listed in this chapter have you never heard of before?

 Do you agree with the open-ended approach to gifts?

 Do you believe that other gifts besides those listed in this chapter exist? If so, what are they?

Notes

1. Ray C. Stedman, *Body Life* (Ventura, CA: Regal Books, 1972), pp. 40-41.
2. Bill Gothard, source unknown.

Four Pitfalls
to Avoid

This is supposed to be a motivational book. My purpose is to get as many believers excited about spiritual gifts as I can. Naturally, I want to be as positive as possible. But at the same time, I am realistic enough to know that churches and believers who embrace biblical ideas of spiritual gifts can easily get sidetracked. Let's not allow this to happen. Let's understand the possible pitfalls.

Through the years, I have observed four significant areas in which dysfunctional ideas about spiritual gifts have been promulgated. While I would not categorize any of them as heresies, I would suggest that they are dangerous pathways that should be avoided. Let me list them first; then I will go into more detail. The four pitfalls that can reduce the effectiveness of ministry through spiritual gifts are these: (1) a short list of gifts, (2) the situational view of spiritual gifts, (3) gift exaltation and (4) gift projection.

GEORGE BARNA'S WAKE-UP CALL

I'm not an alarmist by nature, but I have become alarmed about trends concerning spiritual gifts. George Barna, lauded by many as the foremost researcher of the Christian Church today, has released some startling survey information. When I read it, it was a wake-up call for me. I must confess that during the decade of the 1990s, I had put teaching spiritual gifts on the back burner. But I no longer can do this. God used Barna's research to speak to me clearly about teaching this subject much more. In fact, this book is one of the immediate outcomes. I must have thought that my first book on the subject, *Your Spiritual Gifts Can Help Your Church Grow,* would keep the Church moving in the right direction all by itself. When Barna's report came out, I immediately saw how wrong I was.

First, and most disturbing, George Barna found that a remarkable number of born-again Christians who have heard of spiritual gifts do not think they themselves have been given any spiritual gifts at all. And unfortunately, this number is growing.

Here are the facts: In 1995 the percentage of born-again adults who did not think that they had a spiritual gift was 4 percent. Not too alarming, I would say. But by 2000 that number had risen to 21 percent! Very alarming! If this trend continues, we will soon have a dangerously sick Body on our hands!

Second, Barna found that too many Christians had bizarre ideas of what spiritual gifts really were. They thought that some of the gifts were, for example, a sense of humor or going to church or a good personality or the ability to write poetry or the ability to survive or friendliness or other things that were far from what the Bible teaches.[1]

THE STATE OF THE CHURCH

George Barna's responsibility is to get the facts. Others of us are responsible for interpreting these facts and discovering what is going on. As I worked on processing Barna's data, I came to some conclusions. I will be the first to admit that I may not see the full picture, but I do believe that it is important for me to share my thoughts, realizing that they might be a bit unpopular in certain circles.

Between 1995 and 2000, the churches belonging to what I call the New Apostolic Reformation became the fastest-growing group of churches in the United States.[2] While these churches have tremendous strengths, unfortunately, with some exceptions, their teaching and practice designed to mobilize their church members to do the work of the ministry through spiritual gifts are surprisingly weak. If this observation is correct, it would explain, at least to a considerable extent, Barna's conclusions.

Where does this weakness come from? The genealogy of the New Apostolic Reformation goes back to the independent charismatic movement. The genealogy of the independent charismatic movement goes back to classical Pentecostalism. We will be forever thankful for the role that classical Pentecostalism has played in surfacing the true biblical view of the person and work of the Holy Spirit, the third Person of the Trinity. The kingdom of God would never be where it is today if it weren't for our Pentecostal pioneers in the early part of the last century.

However, while Pentecostals helped us become aware that spiritual gifts were for today, they also incorporated two serious errors concerning spiritual gifts in their teachings. These errors were perpetuated by many independent charismatic leaders and they have also carried over to many New Apostolic Reformation leaders. If we do not correct these two errors, which are the first two of the four pitfalls in this chapter, I believe that the Church will soon be on a downhill slide.

What are these two serious errors?

The Short List of Spiritual Gifts

Classical Pentecostalism teaches that there are nine gifts of the Holy Spirit, all found in the first part of 1 Corinthians 12. They would include wisdom, knowledge, faith, healing, miracles, prophecy, discerning of spirits, tongues and interpretation of tongues. Pentecostal leaders encourage believers to use spiritual gifts, but their teaching and writing on spiritual gifts deal only with this short list, not with the 28 that I listed in the previous chapter.

While these nine gifts are essential for the saints to do the work of the ministry, there are many other functions of the Body of Christ that are also necessary for it to operate as God designed it. Believers who think that there are only nine gifts and who do not happen to minister regularly in any of them will likely be among Barna's 21 percent who think they have no gift at all. They may actually be ministering in one or more of the other 19 gifts such as hospitality or administration or teaching or helps, but they have not been taught to recognize any of these as legitimate spiritual gifts. Consequently, when the interviewer says, "Do you have a spiritual gift?" they will say, "No, I don't think so."

The Situational View of Spiritual Gifts

Classical Pentecostalism has taught that all of the spiritual gifts (all nine, that is) are available to all believers depending on the immediate situation. The hypothesis is that, if you are filled with the Holy Spirit, you will have all the gifts available, since the Holy Spirit has all the gifts. If a situation should arise when prophecy or healing or wisdom or any other gift would be useful, God will activate that gift in any believer. But when that situation passes, the believer might not use the same gift ever again or they might get it only occasionally. This is known as the situational view.

A quick review of the last couple of chapters will show that the situational view is not biblical. The biblical teaching is that our spiritual gifts are like members of our human body. Members of the body such as ears or necks or stomachs or vocal chords are not ears or necks or stomachs or vocal chords for a one-time use or to be used only occasionally. They are constitutionally parts of the body as long as the body is healthy. The view that I am teaching in this book is the *constitutional* view of spiritual gifts as opposed to the *situational* view.

I think I can explain quite briefly how this pitfall crept into classical Pentecostalism years ago. Once Pentecostals started believing in and teaching the baptism in the Holy Spirit, many believers began speaking in tongues. History shows that the early Pentecostal leaders were typically not among those who cared to spend much time in biblical exegesis or theologizing. They knew that tongues was called a spiritual gift, so they assumed that everyone who spoke in tongues must have the gift of tongues. Not a few Pentecostal believers, in fact, ended up speaking in tongues only once in their lives. So the conclusion was that they must have received the gift of tongues for only that one situation. This situational view was subsequently applied to the other eight gifts on the list as well. When later generations produced Pentecostal biblical scholars, they searched and found arguments to justify the position of their predecessors, and the idea became entrenched.

The situational view of spiritual gifts could easily have been avoided if Pentecostal leaders had understood the important distinction between spiritual gifts and Christian roles. I will detail this in the next chapter as a much better way to explain why some believers speak in tongues all the time (the gift) and others perhaps only once (the role).

The situational approach to spiritual gifts, especially when applied to only nine of the gifts, will weaken the Church internally. I remember hearing from a new apostolic leader a sermon entitled "How to Flow in the Nine Gifts of the Holy Spirit." This sermon, judging by its title, combined the two errors of classical

Pentecostalism that have been perpetuated in much of the New Apostolic Reformation today: that there are only nine gifts and that every Spirit-filled believer has them and should use them. If you are a believer who does not prophesy or discern spirits or speak in tongues or do miracles, you would probably tell a Barna researcher that you do not think that you have a spiritual gift.

Fortunately, George Barna has brought to the public eye some of the disturbing effects of this teaching—in time for it to be corrected, I hope.

SPIRITUAL GIFTS: LIFETIME POSSESSIONS

The situational view of spiritual gifts begs the question of how long we keep a spiritual gift once God gives it to us.

In my opinion, once a person is given a bona fide spiritual gift, it is a lifetime possession. This is the constitutional view. I derive it from Romans 12:4, where, once again, Paul gives us the analogy of the physical body as the hermeneutical key for understanding spiritual gifts. If spiritual gifts are to the Body of Christ as, let's say, spinal columns or skin or other members are to the physical body, there is little question in my mind that once we know what our gift is, we can depend on keeping it. For example, I do not go to bed at night having any worry whatsoever that tomorrow my hand might wake up being a kidney. Both the development of the spiritual gifts in the life of an individual Christian and the smooth operation of the Body of Christ as a whole need to depend on similar confidence—confidence that you and I have, and will continue to have, our God-given spiritual gifts.

However, this does not mean that the gifts we have today will necessarily be the sum total of the gifts we have the rest of our lives. God gives us our initial gifts when we are born again. But later in life we might discover that we have and are using gifts that we never used before. There are two ways to explain this. Either we always had the gift and it just surfaced, or God decided to give us a new gift. I personally think that both of these things are likely to happen. For example, I know that I now have the gifts of healing, giving and apostle, but 20 years ago I had no awareness of possessing any of these three gifts.

My point is that we should always be open to moving in new areas of ministry as God determines. We should never become stuck in the mud, so to speak.

DOMINANT AND SUBORDINATE GIFTS

Multigifted people may find that during certain seasons of their ministry, some of their gifts will be dominant and others subordinate. This ranking order might vary over the years as circumstances change. In my opinion, however, this does not mean that a gift has been lost along the way. I know that I have the gift of missionary, for example; but, while it was dominant during my 16 years as a missionary to Bolivia, it has been relatively dormant ever since.

At the same time, there is a danger that some gifts may become dormant contrary to God's will. You may have a gift that you are supposed to be using but are not. This seemed to be what Paul had in mind when he had to keep exhorting Timothy: "Do not neglect the gift" (1 Tim. 4:14) and "stir up the gift" (2 Tim. 1:6) and "do the work of an evangelist" (2 Tim. 4:5), on the obvious assumption that one of Timothy's spiritual gifts was the gift of evangelist. Allowing gifts to become dormant is one of the ways we are in danger of "quench[ing] the Spirit" (1 Thess. 5:19), and we need to avoid that at all costs.

ABUSE OF SPIRITUAL GIFTS

We need to face the unfortunate fact that spiritual gifts can be abused. In a short book like this, I will not attempt to catalog and comment on all the abuses of spiritual gifts common today. We have already discussed the pitfalls of *a short list of gifts* and the *situational view of spiritual gifts*, but I also want to name and comment on two of them that I consider to be especially widespread and counterproductive in the Church. These are pitfalls three and four.

Gift Exaltation

The third pitfall is *gift exaltation*. In some circles, it is popular to exalt one gift over the others. Having a certain gift seems to constitute a spiritual status symbol in some groups. First-class citizens tend to be separated from second-class citizens on the basis of exercising a certain gift or a certain combination of gifts.

When this happens, gifts can easily become ends in themselves rather than means to an end. They can glorify the user rather than the giver. They can benefit the individual more than the Body. They can produce pride and self-indulgence.

A prominent biblical example was the Corinthian church, which had fallen into this trap. They had been exalting the gift of tongues, a very common practice in some churches today. Paul actually writes 1 Corinthians 12–14 in an attempt to scold them and to straighten them out. Their enthusiasm over tongues had caused them to neglect prophecy. The details are not necessary to repeat, but the lesson is that all of us need to take fair warning and avoid gift exaltation.

The Syndrome of Gift Projection

The fourth pitfall is *gift projection*.

Most Christians who have biographies written about themselves have accomplished extraordinary things during their lifetimes. What gave them the ability to turn in the kind of life-time performance that would justify a biography? It has to be that God had given them a spiritual gift or a gift-mix in an unusual degree, that they developed their gifts conscientiously and that they used them to the glory of God and for the benefit of the Body of Christ in a notable way.

Few biographers, however, and few heroes of their biographies have been people who are sensitive to the biblical teaching on spiritual gifts. Rarely do biographers attribute the feats of their heroes to the fact that God had simply gifted them in an unusual way. This has caused them to take another approach toward explaining the cause of their hero's accomplishments. What frequently happens is that readers are led to believe that so-and-so accomplished extraordinary things simply because that person loved God so much and was so obedient. What does this mean? It means that if you only loved God that much, dear reader, and if you only decided to obey Him, you could do the same thing. If you fall short, you now know the reason why. Something must be deficient in your relationship with God.

However, many Christians who read these biographies are, in fact, totally consecrated to God. They are not suffering from spiritual deficiencies. Because of this, they are often the ones who feel the most frustrated, guilty and defeated when they learn about these giants of the faith. To make matters worse, when the heroes of the biographies are ignorant of spiritual gifts, they sometimes engage in what I call gift projection. They seem to say, "Look, I'm just an ordinary Christian, no different from anyone else. Here's what I do, and God blesses it. Consequently, if you just do what I do, God will bless you in the same way." What they rarely say, unfortunately, is "I can do what I do because God has given me a certain gift or gift-mix. If you discover that God has given you the same, join me in this. If not, I don't expect you to be like me. You do what God has equipped you to do, and we will love and support each other as different members of the Body."

People caught up in the syndrome of gift projection seem to want the whole body to be an eye. They unwittingly impose guilt and shame on fellow Christians who are not like them. They tend to make feet say, "Because I am not a hand, I am not of the body" (1 Cor. 12:15). They usually have little idea of how devastating gift projection can be for those who have different gifts. They would be like the steward in the parable who came back with 10 talents saying to the one who came back with 4, "If you only loved the master more, you would have come back with 10 also," without mentioning that the master gave him 5 talents to start with but gave the other only 2 (see Matt. 25:14-30).

Today, more than ever before, we need a healthy, biblical view of spiritual gifts. Let's begin by avoiding the common pitfalls and moving strongly ahead according to God's design for the Body of Christ.

MAKING IT PERSONAL

➔ Have you ever believed, or do you now believe, that you do not possess any spiritual gifts?

➔ Do you agree that once a believer receives a spiritual gift, he or she will always have that spiritual gift? Why or why not?

➔ How do you feel when you hear or read about a person who is unusually gifted?

Notes

1. Barna Research Group, "Awareness of Spiritual Gifts Is Changing," news release, February 5, 2001, pp. 1-2.
2. For details on the New Apostolic Reformation, see my books *The New Apostolic Churches* (Ventura, CA: Regal Books, 1998), *Churchquake!* (Ventura, CA: Regal Books, 1999) and *Changing Church* (Ventura, CA: Regal Books, 2004).

CHAPTER FIVE

Clearing Away
the Confusion

As we go about discovering, developing and using our spiritual gifts, it is important to keep a clear head. Almost every time that I teach on spiritual gifts, I find that certain questions come from the class almost as soon as I begin. These questions can be grouped into four areas of confusion that frequently arise in the process. They relate to (1) natural talents, (2) the fruit of the Spirit (3) Christian roles and (4) counterfeit gifts. Let's look at them one at a time.

DON'T CONFUSE SPIRITUAL GIFTS WITH NATURAL TALENTS

Every human being, by virtue of being made in the image of God, possesses certain natural talents. As with spiritual gifts, we can expect the natural talents to have different variations and degrees. Talents are one of the features that give every human being a unique personality. Part of our self-identity is inevitably wrapped up in the particular mix of talents we have.

Where do these natural talents come from? Ultimately, of course, they are given by God. Consequently, in the broadest sense of the word, they should be recognized as God-given "gifts." That is why we often say of a person who sings well or who has an extraordinary IQ or who can hit a golf ball into a hole from a long distance: "My, isn't that person gifted?" By this, however, we should not imply that they have *spiritual* gifts.

Please be aware that possessing certain natural talents has nothing directly to do with being a Christian or being a member of the Body of Christ. Many Muslims or Hindus or atheists, for example, have superb talents for art or medicine or literature or other things. They have natural talents, but, keep in mind that they do not have *spiritual gifts*. And the ultimate source of these talents, of course, is God the Creator.

Years ago when I was living in the Los Angeles area, the Los Angeles Lakers were dominating the world of professional basketball. One of their players, Kareem Abdul-Jabbar, had an incredible talent for throwing the basketball into the hoop. No NBA player has ever scored more points in a lifetime than he did. At the same time, another one of the Lakers, A. C. Green, had a similar talent. So here is the point. Kareem Abdul-Jabbar was a committed Muslim. A. C. Green was a committed, witnessing Christian, a member of the Body of Christ. Their choice of whom to worship had nothing to do with those natural talents. In fact, day in and day out, the Muslim actually scored more than the Christian.

While Christians, like Muslims or anyone else, have natural talents, these talents should not be confused with spiritual gifts. It is technically incorrect and unbiblical for Christians to say that their gift is fixing automobiles, gourmet cooking, telling jokes, painting pictures or playing basketball.

What Does "Charisma" Mean?

To make matters worse, the biblical Greek word *charisma* has been secularized. I understand that in Greek literature the apostle Paul is the only known author who uses "charisma" frequently. The only other recorded appearances of "charisma" in Greek literature, if I understand it correctly, are in 1 Peter 4:10 and once in Philo's writings. But a century ago a famous German sociologist, Max Weber, began to use the word "charisma" to describe a certain kind of dynamic leader, whom he called a charismatic leader. His word "charismatic" had no theological overtones. In Weber's sense, the word has continued to be used in secular circles. Sociologists would regard Adolf Hitler or Joseph Stalin or the Dalai Lama as having charisma, in the broad sense of the word. But none of the three, as far as I know, would have considered himself a member of the Body of Christ, and thus none of them was given a spiritual gift.

Can Talents Become Gifts?

Why could Hitler, Stalin and the Dalai Lama not have a spiritual gift? Because spiritual gifts are reserved exclusively for Christians. No unbeliever has one, and every true believer in Jesus does. Spiritual gifts are not to be regarded as dedicated natural talents. However, natural talents and spiritual gifts may have a discernible relationship between each other, because in many cases (not all, by any means) God may take an unbeliever's natural talent and transform it into a spiritual gift when that person is saved and becomes a member of the Body of Christ. But in such a case the spiritual gift is more than just a souped-up natural talent. Because it is given by God, a spiritual gift can never be cloned.

Consider, for example, the natural talent of teaching. A significant segment of the population are teachers by profession. But as most every pastor knows, not every well-trained, competent public-school teacher turns out to be a good Sunday School teacher. Why? In those cases, God evidently did not choose to transform the *talent* of teaching into the *gift* of teaching. But in many other cases He does that very thing, and certain school teachers turn out to become excellent Sunday School teachers.

While God frequently transforms a natural talent into a spiritual gift, at the same time many spiritual gifts will have nothing to do with a person's recognized natural talent. I mentioned a while back that I have a gift of healing. Nothing in my background as an unbeliever would have hinted that this would happen. To cite another example, as I write this, one of the most famous public speakers in our country is Benny Hinn. Did you know that when Benny was an unbeliever, he had a serious speech impediment? His eloquence as a preacher, then, was a completely new thing that God did for him after he was saved. The spiritual gift did not connect at all with the natural talent, in Benny Hinn's case.

DON'T CONFUSE SPIRITUAL GIFTS WITH THE FRUIT OF THE SPIRIT

The fruits of the Spirit are listed in Galatians 5:22-23: "love, joy, peace, longsuffering, kindness, goodness, faithfulness, gentleness, self-control." Some Bible expositors point out that "fruit" is in the singular and that the original Greek construction would permit a colon after "love." So although all these other things are part of the fruit of the Spirit, love could well be the primary and all-inclusive one.

Notice that in the list of 28 spiritual gifts in chapter 3, none of them is love. Why? Love is not a spiritual gift. It would be improper to speak of the "gift of love," if by "gift" we meant that love should be seen as spiritual gift number 29 on our list. In the broad sense, of course, love is a gift from God and should be so regarded. "We love [God] because He first loved us" (1 John 4:19). But love is not a charisma in the sense that God gives it to some members of the Body but not to others. No. All believers who have the Holy Spirit should manifest the fruit of the Holy Spirit in their daily lives.

The fruit of the Spirit is the normal, expected outcome of Christian growth, maturity, holiness, Christlikeness and fullness of the Holy Spirit. Because all Christians have the responsibility of growing in their faith, all have the responsibility of developing the fruit. The fruit is not *discovered*, as are the gifts; it is *developed* through the believer's walk with God and through yielding to the Holy Spirit. Although spiritual gifts help define what a Christian *does*, the fruit of the Spirit helps define what a Christian *is*.

The Mess at Corinth

The Corinthian believers found this out the hard way. They had an ideal gift-mix, according to 1 Corinthians 1:7, which says, "You come short in no gift." They were busy discovering, developing and using their spiritual gifts. They were about as charismatic as a church could get. Yet at the same time they were a spiritual disaster area, one of the most messed-up churches we read about in the New Testament.

How can a church be filled with born-again believers, excited about all the spiritual gifts, and still be impotent in the sight of God? If it doesn't have the fruit of the Spirit along with the gifts, it can be.

The basic problem of the Corinthians, therefore, was not gifts, but the fruit. That is why Paul wrote 1 Corinthians 13 to them. In it, he waxed eloquent about love, a fruit of the Spirit. He told them that they might have the gift of tongues, the gift of prophecy, the gift of knowledge, the gift of faith, the gift of voluntary poverty, the gift of martyrdom and any other gift, but without love—fruit—the gifts amounted to absolutely nothing (see 1 Cor. 13:1-3). Gifts without fruit are like an automobile tire without air—the ingredients may be all together, but they are worthless and they will not do what they are intended to do.

Here is the principle: *The fruit of the Spirit is the indispensable foundation for the effective exercise of spiritual gifts.*

Eternal Fruit

Keep in mind also that gifts are temporal, but fruit is eternal. In 1 Corinthians 13 we are also told that gifts such as prophecy, tongues and knowledge will vanish away, but faith, hope and love will abide. Whereas gifts are task oriented, the fruit is God oriented.

It is worth noting that a passage on the fruit of the Spirit accompanies every one of the four primary passages on gifts. First Corinthians 13 is the most explicit and most widely recognized, following 1 Corinthians 12, where the gifts are featured. But also, the list of gifts ending in Romans 12:8 is immediately followed by "let love be without hypocrisy" and "be kindly affectionate to one another with brotherly love" (vv. 9-10). The passage on fruit continues for another 11 verses. Then in Ephesians 4, the gift passage ends with verse 16 and the fruit passage picks up in the next verse and continues into the next chapter. Among other things it says, "Walk in love, as Christ also has loved us" (5:2). Similarly, the passage on spiritual gifts beginning with 1 Peter 4:9 is immediately preceded with "above all things have fervent love for one another, for 'love will cover a multitude of sins' " (v. 8).

DON'T CONFUSE SPIRITUAL GIFTS WITH CHRISTIAN ROLES

When we look at the list of 28 gifts, it becomes obvious that many of them describe characteristics expected of all Christians, whether they have those particular gifts or not. At this point, it is necessary to distinguish between *spiritual gifts* and *Christian roles*. Roles are slightly different from the fruit of the Spirit in that they involve more doing than being. But they are similar to the fruit in that they are characteristic of every conscientious Christian.

You have a spiritual gift, as I have previously explained in detail, because God has chosen to give you that gift once you become a member of the Body of Christ. You have certain Christian roles simply because you are born again and your new nature causes you to do certain things that are expected of you as well as every other believer. Let's look at several examples.

Faith

Perhaps the most obvious spiritual gift that relates directly to a Christian role is faith. Just becoming a Christian and first entering into the Body of Christ requires faith. No one can be a Christian without faith. And this faith, according to the Bible, is a gift of God (see Eph. 2:8-9). Then we are later told that faithfulness is a part of the fruit of the Spirit (see Gal. 5:22) and that "without faith it is impossible to please [God]" (Heb. 11:6). In other words, the lifestyle of every Christian, without exception, is to be characterized by day-in, day-out faith. This is our *role* of faith.

Over and above this, however, the spiritual *gift* of faith (see 1 Cor. 12:9) is given by God to relatively few members of the

Body. This *gift* of faith is much more than the *fruit* of faith or the *role* of faith, both of which we expect to see in every true Christian. I love to be around those with the gift of faith, even though I have never suspected that I was personally gifted in that area. One thinks immediately of those such as George Müller or Bill Bright, whose lives of faith were several notches above the faith that is expected of ordinary believers.

Hospitality

The gift of hospitality provides another example of this difference. Neither my wife, Doris, nor I have that particular gift. We are happiest in our home when no one else is around. Our personality tests show that neither one of us is sanguine (on the Florence Littauer model) or a high "C" (on the DISC model). However, we do have a *role* of entertaining guests in our home, and we do it with some regularity. Having people over for dinner, occasionally putting up a person for the night, taking a visitor on an outing, hosting parties, loaning our car and making sure that new people are oriented to the community are all included in our Christian roles. None of these things comes easily to us and we are aware that we do not do it as often or as well as we should. But we do make a conscientious effort, because doing it is simply part of living the life of a good Christian, part of our Christian role.

Giving

I believe that another role of all Christian believers is to tithe their income to God's work. I am appalled when I read statistics that show that American church members average under 3 percent of their income in giving. Ten percent, biblically speaking, is only a starting point, because that amount does not even belong to us—it belongs to God. Using God's money for ourselves is a serious sin. It amounts to robbing God and it even brings a curse, according to Malachi 3:8-9. True giving only starts with our offerings from the 90 percent that God has given to us. What I'm saying here is that tithing is not a spiritual gift, nor is giving offerings above that—these are Christian roles.

There is also a spiritual gift of giving, as we see in Romans 12:8. The believers who have this gift habitually give a percentage of their income far higher than the 10 percent plus that God expects of those who do not have the gift. Years ago, for example, Doris and I decided that if the government requires a graduated income tax, we should also give a graduated tithe to the Lord's work. So we determined that each year that our income went up, we would raise the percentage of what we give. This has now brought us into a tithe bracket far higher than we ever imagined, and we continue to give cheerfully. However, I realize that it would be spiritually arrogant of me to say to others that they should do the same. Why? Because we know that it is God who has chosen to give us the gift of giving, and that most others do not have the same gift.

Prayer and Other Gifts and Roles

Prayer is another example of a Christian role. Prayer, of course, is the privilege and responsibility of every Christian. No special spiritual gift is needed for a vital prayer life. One does not need the gift of intercession to talk to God on a regular basis, but some have been given a gift of intercession and they have a prayer relationship with God that far exceeds what most of us experience on a regular basis. Spending two, three, four, five hours or more in prayer every day is part of a typical intercessor's lifestyle.

Let me mention a few others: Some have the spiritual gift of service, but nevertheless all Christians should serve one another (see Gal. 5:13). Some have the spiritual gift of exhortation, but all believers have a general role of exhorting one another (see Heb. 10:25). A few have the gift of evangelist, but all Christians are expected to exercise their role of being a witness for Christ (see Acts 1:8).

The Constitutional View of Gifts

Let's go back to George Barna's research, which I mentioned several times in chapter 4. His research showed that the level of understanding of spiritual gifts among born-again adults has been decreasing since 1995. I suggested in chapter 4 that one of the reasons why ignorance of spiritual gifts is on the increase in the American church may be the influence of the *situational* over the *constitutional* view of spiritual gifts. I also suggested that one way to avoid the unbiblical situational view is to understand the difference between spiritual gifts and Christian roles. Now let me explain in a bit more detail.

I know one prominent pastor who wanted power healing to be a prominent feature of the life and ministry of his church. He did not care to be seen as a superstar faith healer, but rather he wanted to equip all the believers in his church to lay hands on the sick, pray for them and see them healed. This is the good news. The bad news is that he erroneously thought that in order to do this, all the believers in his church needed the spiritual gift of healing. Consequently, he switched from the constitutional view of spiritual gifts, which he had been teaching for years, to the situational view. He wanted healing so badly that he fell into the common error of supposing that the whole body could be an eye (see 1 Cor. 12:17). This unbiblical approach reduced the water level of ministering with all 28 spiritual gifts. The healing ministry of the church did have a good surge, but it subsequently could not be sustained. That church today sees no more healing than an average church would.

It would have been much better, in my opinion, to have taught the people that every one of them had a Christian role of laying hands on the sick and praying for their healing, just like they had a role of giving tithes and offerings, of interceding for others or of being a good witness to unbelievers. None of these things requires a gift. Nevertheless, God does give spiritual gifts of healing, giving, intercession and evangelist to certain members of the Body whom He chooses. This is the biblical formula for a healthy church.

If believers think that they will be given any and all of the gifts according to the situation they find themselves in, their minds tend to become closed to the possibility that God will give them one or more gifts for which they need to take the responsibility to develop and use on a consistent basis. If believers take the situational approach, they can too easily fall into the 21 percent reflected in Barna's research who do not think that they have any real spiritual gift at all. This erroneous belief weakens the whole Body of Christ.

DON'T CONFUSE SPIRITUAL GIFTS WITH COUNTERFEIT GIFTS

I wish I did not have to write this section on counterfeit gifts. I wish it were not true that Satan and his demons and evil spirits are real and actively opposing the work of the Lord. Jesus Himself said, "For false christs and false prophets will rise and show great signs and wonders, so as to deceive, if possible, even the elect" (Matt. 24:24). Jesus also spoke about those who prophesy and cast out demons in His name but who, in reality, turn out to be workers of iniquity (see 7:22-23).

I do not doubt that Satan can and does counterfeit every gift on the list. He is a supernatural being and he has supernatural powers—powers that originate in the realm of darkness. Satan's power was shown in a spectacular way in Egypt when Pharaoh's magicians could publicly match some of the supernatural works that God did through Moses (see Exod. 7—8). Of course, Satan's power is limited and controlled. In Egypt he could match God's works only to a certain point, and this applies today as well.

A rather chilling book on this subject, entitled *The Challenging Counterfeit*, was written by Raphael Gasson, now a Christian but formerly a spiritualist medium. He tells it like it is out there in the real world. Gasson's experience has shown him that "it is very obvious that Satan is using an extremely subtle counterfeit to the precious gifts of the Spirit."[1] In his book, Gasson describes in detail several of Satan's favorite counterfeits.

False Gifts

Gasson specifically shows, for example, how false gifts of faith, miracles, healing, tongues and the interpretation of tongues are produced by Satan. The counterfeit of the gift of discerning spirits, he feels, is clairvoyance and clairaudience. The gift of deliverance is cleverly reproduced by the devil as well, and this is one of the reasons I do not like to refer to it as the gift of exorcism.

Gasson also recalls how Satan gave him, as he gives to many other fortune-tellers, the ability to prophesy, and points out that most of these counterfeit prophecies came true. This is one way the devil makes his appeals more attractive. Psychics can earn a living by receiving information from the invisible world through agents of the devil.

On one occasion during the World War II years, for example, a man brought to Gasson an item belonging to the man's son who was in the military. The man wanted to find out where his son was. Through his "spirit guide," who purported to be the spirit of an African witch doctor, Gasson found out that the owner of the item was well and a prisoner of war. The father then proceeded to show Gasson a telegram from the War Department stating that his son had been killed in action more than two weeks previously. Gasson went back to his guide and verified that the soldier-son really was not dead and that the father would have this confirmed in three days. Sure enough, three days later the father received a telegram from the War Department apologizing for the mistake and saying that the boy was well and a prisoner of war.

Some people mistakenly interpret this kind of prophecy as a work of God. It is in reality the clever counterfeit of the devil. But as we have just seen, it is no less real.

We immediately need to remind ourselves that God knows all about this deceitfulness and that He has given adequate power to His children to prevent it. For example, one of my colleagues on the Lausanne Committee for World Evangelization some years ago was Petrus Octavianus of Indonesia. On one occasion, Petrus was speaking to an audience of 3,000 people in Stuttgart, Germany. At the end of his presentation, he asked for a time of silent prayer. When all was quiet, one man on the platform got up and began praying in tongues. Petrus Octavianus turned to him and in the name of Jesus commanded him to be silent. Octavianus later explained, "After I had prayed for clarity, it became clear to me that this speaking in tongues was not brought about by the Holy Spirit but by the enemy." It turned out to be true and the man was exposed as a fraud.

Discernment of Spirits

How do we deal with such counterfeits? The Body needs the gift of discernment of spirits, which operates like the white corpuscles in the human body. The white corpuscles build our immune system by detecting and attacking pathological invaders. The definition of the gift of discernment of spirits is this: *The special ability that God gives to certain members of the Body of Christ to know with assurance whether certain behaviors purported to be of God are in reality divine, human or satanic.*

Let me illustrate by going back a few years to when I was teaching the 120 Fellowship, an adult Sunday School class at Lake Avenue Church in Pasadena, California. We regularly had around 100 adults of all ages. The custom was to have coffee together before we sat down at tables for the teaching time. One Sunday I introduced myself to this nice, attractive lady at the coffee urn. She told me that she had been looking forward to coming to class for quite a while, but that this was the first time she was able to make it, and that she was really excited about being there. That made me feel quite good. When I started to teach, she was seated at a table toward my left and my wife, Doris, was seated at one toward my right.

I was teaching along, just as I always did, supposing that everything was normal. Then suddenly, that new lady got up from her chair and, she did not walk, she ran out the door! We never saw her again.

What had happened? Doris, who has done deliverance ministry for years, has the gift of discernment of spirits. When the class got under way, she discerned that the nice-looking lady on the other side of the room was, in reality, a witch who had come to curse the class. She engaged the spirits who were operating through the witch, and the lady knew she had met her match, that her cover was blown, and that she was in the wrong place at the wrong time!

Since I don't have the gift of discernment of spirits, I need others around me who do, and I am very fortunate to be married to Doris, who protects me in some ways that I know and, I'm sure, in many other ways that I never know about.

It is essential to keep in mind that "He who is in you is greater than he who is in the world" (1 John 4:4). Knowing that Satan is active should not end up making us timid. We receive spiritual gifts from God Himself as He fills us with the Holy Spirit. He will overrule all the efforts of the enemy to confuse us about our true, bona fide spiritual gifts. God is determined that you, and every other true member of the Body of Christ, will fulfill the destiny that He has for you through fruitful ministry with your spiritual gifts.

MAKING IT PERSONAL

→ How would you describe the difference between a natural talent and a spiritual gift?

→ Why is the fruit of the Spirit important when using the spiritual gifts?

→ What are some specific Christian roles that you have practiced?

→ How does God help believers discern between genuine and counterfeit gifts?

Note

1. Raphael Gasson, *The Challenging Counterfeit* (Plainfield, NJ: Logos International, 1979), p. 90.

CHAPTER SIX

The Five Steps
for Discovering Your Spiritual Gifts

Nowhere does the Bible deal specifically with finding gifts. Nowhere does Peter or Paul or James say, "And now, brethren, I would have you follow these steps to discover your spiritual gifts." The lack of such a passage has convinced some Christians that discovering gifts is an improper pursuit. I disagree.

In my opinion, the lack of such specific instructions in the Bible should not be a deterrent to set forth practical, twenty-first-century procedures for knowing and doing God's will. Nowhere does the Bible tell us how to draw up the constitution and bylaws for a local church or what church membership requirements should be. Nowhere does the Bible tell us how to organize a missionary-sending agency or how to support missionaries. For centuries, theologians and Bible students have been trying to determine exactly when and how Christians should be baptized. Most Christians do not regard these things as major stumbling blocks.

On this particular issue of spiritual gifts, I am not alone. Most authors of current books on spiritual gifts include information on how to discover one's gift. Most of them, in fact, are saying just about the same thing. Authors try not to copy each other, so each one develops a different way of saying it. But the procedure for finding gifts is surprisingly similar from author to author. This is comforting, because it does seem that a consensus has been emerging, which helps reduce confusion and increase effectiveness throughout the Church. In any case, we who are in the field of teaching spiritual gifts are much closer to agreement with each other on how to do it than those, for example, who are dealing with issues of baptism or events surrounding the second coming of Christ.

BE MINDFUL OF THE FOUR FUNDAMENTAL PREREQUISITES

Before beginning to take the actual steps toward finding your gift, four fundamental prerequisites need to characterize your life. Leave out any one of them, and you will have a very difficult time discovering your gift.

First, you have to be a Christian. Spiritual gifts are given only to members of the Body of Christ. Unfortunately, not all church members in America are truly members of the Body of Christ. Almost all churches, some more than others, have members who are not personally committed to Jesus. These people may attend church with some regularity, put money in the offering plate and even belong to some boards or committees and teach Sunday School. They may know how to be religious, but they have never come into that personal relationship with the Savior that some call being born again and others call commitment to Christ or being saved or converted. The term used is much less important than the idea it conveys, namely, an actual personal relationship with Jesus Christ.

Second, you have to believe in spiritual gifts. I am almost certain that the reason that some born-again Christians do not believe in spiritual gifts is simply that no one has told them about spiritual gifts. In my experience, I cannot recall any Christian who has seriously listened to teaching on spiritual gifts and has not recognized that these gifts are for today—and for them.

This boils down to a matter of faith. You must *believe* that God has given you a spiritual gift before you start the process of discovering it. Earlier I tried to make the best case possible to prove that every Christian, including you, has one or more spiritual gifts. If you haven't been convinced as yet, the five steps in this chapter may not be for you. For the steps to work, you must have a sense of gratitude to God that He has given you a gift, and a sense of joyful anticipation in finding out what it is.

Third, you have to be willing to work. The five steps I am about to suggest constitute a spiritual exercise, and God's help is needed to accomplish it. Notice that I mentioned God's *help*. Keep in mind that, while God will help you, He doesn't offer to do your work for you. You must take the initiative.

God has given you one or more spiritual gifts for a reason: He has a ministry assignment that He wants you to accomplish in the Body of Christ, a specific job for which He has personally equipped you. God knows whether you are serious about working for Him. If He sees that you just want to discover your gift for the fun of it or because everybody else is doing it or because it gives you some new status, you cannot expect Him to help you very much.

If, however, you promise to use your spiritual gift, whatever it may be, for the glory of God and for the welfare of the Body of Christ, He will definitely help you. Recognize that this is God's best for you. Be open to what He wants to do through you. Discovering gifts is not an ego trip, although it should raise your self-esteem tremendously. If you are ready for a life as an active, productive believer, you are ready for the five steps. They will help you move into your true destiny.

Fourth, you have to pray. Before, during and after this process, you should pray. "If any of you lacks wisdom," James says, "let him ask of God, who gives to all liberally" (Jas. 1:5). Beseech God sincerely and earnestly for His guidance all the way through the five steps. Because God wants you to discover your spiritual gift, He certainly will give you all the help you need. Just ask and believe that He will. He will give you the revelation that will unlock the beautiful possibilities for the fruitful ministry He has already placed within you.

Knowing these four prerequisites, you are ready for the five steps necessary to discover your spiritual gift.

STEP 1: EXPLORE THE POSSIBILITIES

The first step in planning most human endeavors is to consider all the possible options. If you want to travel from Dallas to Philadelphia, for example, you need to know that it can be done by train, airplane, automobile, motorcycle, horseback, hitchhiking, bus and other ways. If you choose to go by land, you look at a map and explore the various possible routes. Then you choose the one that suits you the best. This is normal and logical.

Likewise, it is difficult to discover a spiritual gift if you do not know approximately what you are looking for ahead of time. The purpose of this first step, explore the possibilities, is to become familiar enough with the different gifts that God ordinarily gives to the Body of Christ so that when you come across your gift later on, you will recognize it for what it really is.

Here are five ways to approach this exciting first step.

Study the Bible

Naturally, the basic source of data about the possible spiritual gifts is located in the Bible. Read the major passages on spiritual gifts time and again. Read them in several different versions. Find examples in the lives of good people in the Bible and how these gifts might have worked in practice. Using whatever helps are available, cross-check Scripture references until you feel you are familiar with what they reveal. Check out the glossary of spiritual gifts in the back of this book and read the Scripture references there.

Learn Your Church's Position on Gifts

As I have mentioned several times, by no means is there universal agreement among churches and denominations about which gifts are in operation today. Nor would I expect these differences to be resolved in our lifetimes.

Because I believe strongly in commitment to the Body of Christ, I believe that when a person voluntarily joins a church, he or she ought to be under the discipline and authority of that church. On the matter of spiritual gifts, the major difference between churches today frequently concerns what I have referred to as the sign gifts—namely, speaking in tongues but there are others as well. Some churches expect the gift of tongues to be used in their worship services. Some have special services on a weekday when tongues can be used, but they do not allow it in Sunday worship. Some do not allow tongues to be used in any of the meetings held in the church, but they do not object to it in home cell groups or in private prayer. Other churches are convinced that tongues should not be used at all in our day and age.

Suppose that you determine the position of your church on this and other gifts, but you disagree? I suggest one of two courses of action: Either decide to be loyal to your church and its belief and practice without grumbling, or respectfully leave and ask God to take you to another church where you will feel more at home. Notice that I didn't suggest that you set out to change the point of view of your pastor or other church leaders. Church membership, unlike marriage, is not until death do you part. While I do not recommend chronic church hopping, moving into a church that will allow you to be everything God wants you to be is a good way to go.

I think that, at the end of the day, God is pleased with the variety of gift-mixes being used among different churches and denominations. We need to recognize that we are the way we are, both individually and collectively, largely because God has made us that way. Our Master gives some of His servants two talents and some five, but He expects us to use whatever He gives us to accomplish His purpose.

Read Extensively

Never before have Christian readers had available a richer literary fare on the subject of spiritual gifts. I recommend my more comprehensive book on the subject, *Your Spiritual Gifts Can Help Your Church Grow,* because it includes detailed descriptions of each one of the spiritual gifts. Read other books. List the points where the authors agree on the definition of a particular gift and where they disagree. Put all that together with what you are learning from the Bible and formulate your own opinion. What difference does it really make if I think a certain person's gift is the gift of prophecy and someone else thinks it is the gift of knowledge? God is overseeing the whole issue, and He is probably more broad-minded and more flexible than we think. In most cases, He can use us for His glory just the way we are.

Get to Know Gifted People

Seek out and talk to Christian people who have discovered and developed and are now using their spiritual gift or gifts. Find out how they articulate what their gifts are and how they interpret their ministry through gifts.

Make Gifts a Conversation Piece

Contemporary Christians have come a long way in understanding spiritual gifts, but even so, a large number are still reluctant to talk about them to each other with ease. An attitude exists that says, "If I talk about my spiritual gift, people will think I am bragging" or "If I talk about not having a gift, it's a cop-out." I hope we will shed such inhibitions soon and that we will be able to share openly with each other what our gifts are or what they are not. This will help us and our friends and our children know what the optimum possibilities are for our ministry.

STEP 2: EXPERIMENT WITH AS MANY GIFTS AS YOU CAN

You would never know you had a talent for bowling, for example, if you had not tried it. You would never know you could write poetry if you had never written some. I wonder if I have a talent for hang gliding? I will never know for sure unless I try it.

Obviously, some spiritual gifts do not lend themselves easily to experimentation. I do not know how to suggest an experiment with the gift of martyrdom, for example. Someone said that that is the gift you only use once! Although some gifts may be like that, the majority are not. You can readily experiment with them, and I recommend that you do as much experimenting as possible.

Looking for the Needs

A starting point is to look around and see what needs you can identify. Then try to do something to meet a need. Look for the needs of other people. Look for the needs of the church. Look for needs in the workplace. Find out where you can be useful in any way, and do it.

Be available for any job around the church that you might be asked to do. When you get an assignment, undertake it in prayer. Ask the Lord to show you through that experience whether you might have a spiritual gift along those lines. Hang in there and work hard. Discovering gifts does not usually come quickly. Give each job a fair shake and do not give up easily.

Discovering Which Gifts You Do and Do Not Have

While you are experimenting with the gifts, it is just as important to answer the question, Which gifts *don't* I have? as it is to answer the opposite question, Which gifts *do* I have? Every gift you find you do *not* have reduces the number of options you need to work at for reaching the positive answer.

Let me tell a story that will highlight how important it is to discover, through experimenting, what gift you do *not* have.

When I graduated from Fuller Seminary back in the mid-1950s, I had learned next to nothing about spiritual gifts. I think that evangelical leaders generally were still unsure of the Pentecostal movement at that time and had not yet articulated their own position on the gifts. In those days, we certainly were not taught that we had gifts and that we each needed to discover, develop and use them. After seminary, I was ordained by an evangelical, Bible-believing church, but not one of the seven ministers on my ordaining council asked me whether I had any spiritual gifts or whether I knew what they were. I was accepted and served under two evangelical mission agencies. Neither mission agency asked questions about spiritual gifts on its application form. So I went to Bolivia in 1956 being ignorant of spiritual gifts.

While I did not know much about spiritual gifts, I did know what I wanted to be. Those were the days when Billy Graham had just moved into orbit. He became the hero of many seminary students, including me. I marveled at the way he would preach to a stadium full of people, deliver a simple Bible message, give an invitation and see people get up all over the place, fill the aisles and pour down to the front of the stadium to make a decision for Christ. That was for me! My friends and I would imitate Billy Graham's gestures in our preaching classes. We would hold our Bibles like Billy Graham did. We would try to preach with his North Carolina accent. We learned to articulate "The Bible says . . ." and have appropriate sparks of fire in our eyes.

By the time I was ready to go to the mission field, I had it all figured out. Billy Graham could have America—I would take Bolivia! In my mind, I could see thousands and thousands of Bolivians finding Christ through my messages.

I had to spend some time learning Spanish, of course, but when I did, I was ready to begin. I prepared a beautiful sermon in Spanish and used all the homiletical skills I had learned in seminary. I thought the sermon also had one or two things in it that Billy Graham himself might not have thought of. Then I preached the sermon with all my heart and gave the invitation. Nobody came!

Disappointed and somewhat dejected, I tried to figure out what had happened. Perhaps it had to do with prayer. Even at best I have never been a great prayer warrior, but with all the effort it took me to prepare the sermon that time, I had to admit that I had hardly prayed at all. So I prepared another sermon using the best principles of homiletics. But this time I prayed intensely before I went into the pulpit. The results were the same. Nobody came. People acted as if they were permanently glued to their seats.

I then thought something in my life must be blocking my relationship with the Lord. The consecration theology I was taught had programmed me to feel that I must not properly be presenting my body as "a living sacrifice" (Rom. 12:1), for if I were doing that, certainly God would bless my evangelistic ministry.

My thoughts went back to seminary again. I recalled a professor of personal evangelism who used to keep our class spellbound by telling stories of how God had used him to win others to Christ. He would tell about how he would get on a bus and sit next to a total stranger, and by the time they got off the bus the stranger would have accepted Christ. I was impressed!

So I got on a bus and took a seat next to a total stranger. By the time we got off the bus he was mad at me! I was devastated!

For months and years during that first term of missionary service I went through experience after experience like that. I wanted to be Bolivia's Billy Graham, but something was preventing me.

Then, little by little, I finally began to learn about spiritual gifts. As I matured in that process, one day I made what I now consider one of the most important spiritual discoveries of my Christian life—*God had not given me the gift of evangelist!*

From that day on, I have been a better Christian, a better missionary, a more joyous person, a better husband and father and a more competent servant of God. When I realized that on the Day of Judgment, God is not going to hold me accountable for what I did as an evangelist, I felt liberated. Guilt rolled off like the load on the back of Christian in *Pilgrim's Progress*. It was God Himself who had never wanted me to be the Billy Graham of Bolivia. What a relief!

I had experimented with a spiritual gift. I had tried hard to use it. And I had come to the important discovery that I did not have the gift.

Let me hasten to say that although I may not have the *gift* of evangelist, like every other Christian I do have the *role* of witness. Wherever I go and at all times I try to be a good representative of God. I know how to share Christ, and I occasionally lead people to the Lord. Not having the gift of evangelist should never be a cop-out from our responsibility of consistent witnessing for Christ.

Using the Gifts Inventories

One of the best ways to determine which gifts to experiment with first is to go through the spiritual-gifts questionnaire found in chapter 7. Although a gifts inventory like this should not be considered the final word on discovering gifts, it can be very helpful in pointing you in the right direction. This questionnaire scores each gift from 0 to 15, and I suggest that you begin seriously experimenting with, say, the top 3 or 4 on your list.

As you do, don't forget the two questions: (1) Do I have it? and (2) Don't I have it?

STEP 3: EXAMINE YOUR FEELINGS

Somewhere along the line, personal feelings have fallen into disrepute with many believers. If a person is found to really enjoy life, according to this way of thinking, something must be wrong. But, happily, things are changing. The new teaching on spiritual gifts is opening the way for an age in which serving God can be fun.

My concept is this: The same God who gives spiritual gifts also oversees the way each one of us is made up in our total being. God knows every detail of our psychological condition, our glands and hormones, our metabolism, our total personality. He understands our feelings perfectly. He knows our personality profile. And He also knows that if we enjoy doing a task, we do a better job at it than if we do not enjoy it. So part of God's plan, as I understand it, is to match the spiritual gift He gives us with our temperament in such a way that if we really have a gift, we will feel good using it. I think that this is why God reserves the assigning of spiritual gifts for Himself. All the computers at IBM would not be equipped to assign gifts to the hundreds of millions of believers around the world, but it is no problem to God Almighty.

The Bible also tells us that God wants to lead His people through their desires. Psalm 37:4 says, "Delight yourself also in the LORD, and He shall give you the desires of your heart." Philippians 2:13 adds, "For it is God who works in you both to will and to do for His good pleasure." Apparently, when people are doing God's will, they will be doing what they *want* to do because God has given them that desire. Biblically, then, it is clear that we should not have a conflict between enjoying ourselves and pleasing God.

During that same first term as a missionary, when I discovered that I did not have the gift of evangelist, I also discovered, largely through feelings this time, that I did not have the gift of pastor.

My wife, Doris, and I were assigned by our mission to the small village of San José de Chiquitos, where, among other things, we were to plant a new church. We started the church, small and struggling as it was. But in the course of trying out pastoral work, I learned that I was not well equipped to handle people's personal problems. When someone begins to tell me about his or her personal life, I come unglued. I tend to worry about it, lose sleep over it, want to cry and overreact in many ways. I make all the wrong moves. I cannot trust my intuitions. In short, my feelings tell me that God has not given me the pastoral gift.

Of course I do have the *role* of occasionally helping others through their problems and relating in a pastoral way when certain situations occur. Members of my family, certain friends and, at times, students need my help and I try to give it to them as best as I can. My rate of success at personal counseling, however, is extremely low—somewhat near zero. And because I react so poorly, I tend to avoid counseling situations as much as possible. Some people find it hard to understand that, for those of us who do not have the gift of pastor, listening to others' problems can be a serious drain on our emotional energies.

Even after I had realized that I do not have the gift of pastor, I did accept a pastorate once. An important principle lay behind my acceptance. Sometimes a circumstance will arise when we take on a responsibility for a season simply because it is the right thing to do, not because we necessarily have a gift for it. In my case it meant filling in as pastor of a large city church in Bolivia during the time when the pastor took a year's leave of absence in order to coordinate a massive nationwide evangelistic initiative. At that point I was willing to do what I was called upon to do, although it meant ministering for a time on the basis of a role rather than a gift.

I had been teaching this step about testing your feelings for several years, when a wonderful confirmation came. It turned out that Peyton Marshall, a graduate student in psychology at St. Louis University, did his doctoral dissertation on the Wagner-Modified Houts Questionnaire (the one found in chapter 7 of this book). In it, Marshall suggested that a psychologist could predict to a large extent how a person might score on my questionnaire by how that person scored on a standard psychological profile test. His research provides evidence that God matches the gifts He gives us to our temperament and our personality.

Although feelings may have to be put aside from time to time on the basis of a situation like pastoring that church in Bolivia, it should only be temporary. The normal thing is for believers to feel excited about the work they are doing for God because they have discovered the spiritual gift or gifts that God has given them. While experimenting with the gifts, then, it is important to examine your feelings.

STEP 4: EVALUATE YOUR EFFECTIVENESS

Since spiritual gifts are task oriented toward doing ministry, it is not out of order to expect them to work. If God has given you a gift, He has undoubtedly done so because He wants you to accomplish something for Him in the context of the Body of Christ. Gifted people see results for their efforts. Postulating that God wants you to be successful is not contradictory to sincere Christian humility. If you experiment with a gift and consistently find that what it is supposed to accomplish does not happen, you probably have discovered another one of the gifts that God has not given you.

This is where I got my first clues that I do not have the gift of evangelist. I tried with dedication and sincerity and it simply did not work. I tried public evangelism and I failed. I tried personal evangelism and got knots in my stomach and became tongue-tied. I kept trying to witness to people next to me on airplanes, and I can't remember one whom I succeeded in leading to Christ. When I observed some of my friends who were effortlessly witnessing and leading large numbers of people to Christ, I then knew that, compared to them, I was getting very little supernatural help in evangelizing. I was attempting it in the flesh, not in the Spirit. God was trying to tell me something.

On the other hand, a major reason that I know I have the gift of teaching is that people learn when I teach, whether in classrooms or through my books. I have a high expectation that if you have read this book up to here, you have learned something that you didn't know previously—even if you have read another of my books on spiritual gifts or heard me teach a lesson on the subject. I am not saying this to boast; I am saying it only to point out that the Holy Spirit gives me supernatural help when I teach. I do not detect this kind of help when I attempt to evangelize.

If you have the gift of evangelist, people will come to Christ regularly through your ministry. You will love to evangelize. If you have the gift of exhortation or counseling, you will help people through their problems and see many lives straightened out. If you have the gift of healing, sick people will consistently get well. If you have the gift of administration, the organization will run smoothly. When true gifts are in operation, whatever is supposed to happen through them will happen.

STEP 5: EXPECT CONFIRMATION FROM THE BODY

If you think you have a spiritual gift and you have been trying your best to exercise it but if no one else in your church thinks you have it, you probably do not. A gift needs to be confirmed.

At this point you might sense a conflict between step 4, concerning your feelings, and step 5, concerning confirmation. Feelings are important, but they are far from infallible. You may have a deep desire to help other people, for example. You may feel strongly that God is calling you to minister through counseling or through the gift of exhortation. But if you have been experimenting with counseling and have found that over a period of time very few people seek you out for help or recommend their friends and relatives to you or write notes to you telling how much you have helped them, you have good reason to doubt the validity of your feelings as far as that spiritual gift is concerned. Confirmation from the Body serves as a check on all the other steps. Although I have listed this step last, in some ways it can be the most important of all.

The gifts, according to our definition, are given for use within the context of the Body. It is necessary, then, that other members of the Body have an important say in confirming your gift.

Another reason why confirmation from the Body is so important is that it builds in a system of accountability for the use of gifts. Whereas it is true that we are ultimately accountable to God, more immediately we are accountable to each other, and we need to take this seriously. In the Church we need to act like a team. We need the other players and they need us. Our goals are not individual goals; they are goals of the team.

If you have the gift of administration or helps or hospitality or mercy but nobody else knows it, you may easily fall into the trap of being lazy about using it, thinking that no one will know the difference. But once your gift is known and confirmed by the Body, your friends will rightly expect to see it in action. This is why I pointed out earlier in this chapter that a desire to work hard is a prerequisite for discovering spiritual gifts. When members of the Body confirm one another's gifts, more can be accomplished just on the basis of people working harder at what God has called them to do, and the Church will be healthy.

For some years, I thought I had the gift of administration. Somewhat against my will at first, I was talked into taking over the administration of the mission agency under which Doris and I were serving. As I experimented with administration, I began to enjoy it quite a bit. As far as feelings were concerned, it seemed like it might be a gift. Then when my position would come up for confirmation at the annual field conference meeting, a good bit of disagreement would occur among fellow workers about whether I was the right person for the job. Whenever the vote was taken, I would barely squeak by. Looking back, I now realize that I needed someone who had the gift of exhortation to tell me to get out of administration and go back to teaching, but either that person was not there or I was not listening. So I continued for some years, and predictably, the mission did not advance notably under my management.

Only after I returned to the United States and read *The Making of a Christian Leader,* written by the late Ted Engstrom, did I begin to understand clearly that I never did have the gift of administration. In this case, another member of the Body, Ted, confirmed to me that I did not have the gift, and I have been grateful to him ever since. In fact, that became very important when, later on, Fuller Seminary offered me a promotion to a position of administration and I turned it down because I knew that I did not have the gift for it. And as it turned out, I was much happier teaching.

FIND YOUR SPIRITUAL GIFT!

This chapter has been so autobiographical that an explanation might be in order. As many evangelists have discovered, personal testimonies can be extremely helpful in motivating people, because the testimonies provide something of flesh and blood with which to identify. Abstract concepts are fine, but they rarely move people. My purpose in this chapter has been to help you see more clearly how you can begin the exciting process of discovering your spiritual gift or gifts.

Let me give a final example of how this process can work by quoting a letter from one of the most successful church-growth pastors in the United Methodist Church, Joe Harding. At the time of this incident, Pastor Harding's church, the Central

United Protestant Church of Richland, Washington, was one of the largest and fastest-growing churches of the whole Northwest, an area not particularly known for explosive church growth. Joe Harding had enrolled in a church-growth seminar, which I was teaching in Harding's own church facilities. A few days after I taught my lesson on spiritual gifts, Joe wrote me this letter:

> Your class was particularly helpful to me in making a major decision. Just a few days before the class I had received a telephone call from one of our denominational executives asking me to move to a national office in the Board of Discipleship in Nashville to head up a new program of evangelism. I was told that I was their first choice and they really wanted me to accept this responsibility. I am acquainted with the program and I am enthusiastic about it.
>
> However, as I weighed the matter very carefully it was clear to me that my gifts are not primarily in administration, but in preaching and teaching and in pastoring. When I measured my personal gifts against the requirements of this challenging job, it was very easy for me to decline and to feel that God was calling me to remain in this congregation to demonstrate the potential of dynamic and vital growth within the Methodist church.
>
> I was in agony when I first received the call, because I felt I could not decline such a challenging opportunity. Your emphasis on the joy that you find in exercising the gifts put the matter in an entirely different perspective. I find that tremendous joy in standing before the congregation that I preach to, Sunday after

Sunday. I simply know that that is what God is calling me to do.

So your class came at a most appropriate time in my life and I simply want to share my gratitude with you.[1]

The thrill I felt from receiving Joe Harding's letter could not have been any less than that which Billy Graham must feel when 3,000 people come forward in one of his crusades. I now thank God that I am not the Billy Graham of Bolivia, as I once thought I might be. God had something much better for *me*. He has a similar exciting and fulfilling thing in mind for *you*.

MAKING IT PERSONAL

→   Are there any prerequisites to discovering your spiritual gifts that you have not fulfilled yet? If so, you may want to do them now.

→   What is one step that you have already taken to discover your spiritual gifts?

→   What is one step that you are willing to take? If you haven't already taken the Wagner-Modified Houts Questionnaire, you may want to go to chapter 7 and answer the questions now.

Note
1. Joseph Harding, letter to the author, n.d.

CHAPTER SEVEN

Let's Get Started!

Are you ready to actually begin to discover what spiritual gifts God has given you for your life and your ministry? This chapter will give you a running start.

BEFORE YOU START

You are now about to become involved in an exciting spiritual exercise. You know that God has given you one or more spiritual gifts, and discovering that gift or gifts will be a thrilling experience.

In fact, you may be among those who have known what your spiritual gifts are for some time. When that is the case, and it often is, the questionnaire is not irrelevant. Almost all who take the test are very anxious to see their scores. In most cases, the results will affirm and reinforce what you already know. But many believers have taken the test over a number of years since the questionnaire went into use in the mid-1970s, and through it God has shown them new areas of ministry that He is opening up for them. For the veterans as well as for the novices, this is a stimulating and enjoyable experience!

You will be asked to rate the 135 statements found in the Wagner-Modified Houts Questionnaire. Thousands and thousands of believers have been blessed by using the Wagner-Modified Houts

Questionnaire over the years. Constant feedback from them has enabled me to refine the questionnaire over and over again, to the point where you can be assured that it will give you a fairly accurate picture of what kind of ministry God expects you to be carrying out in your group of believers.

However, do not regard the results of this test as final. The three or four gifts you score highest in may or may not be your real spiritual gifts. But you can be sure in either case that they are a starting point for prayer and experimentation. You will need other members of the Body of Christ to help you confirm what gifts you have.

I have omitted the gift of martyrdom from the questionnaire because, after several attempts, I still could not find a valid way to test for it. The test results kept indicating that about 30 percent of believers had the gift of martyrdom, and I could not make much sense out of those numbers. What this means is that the questionnaire tests for only 27 out of the 28 spiritual gifts listed in this book.

There is an obvious shortcoming to the questionnaire. The answers, as you will see, are based on your personal experience. Consequently, if you are a new believer or a young person, you probably do not have much of a track record in ministry to go on. You will enjoy the experience, but hold the results lightly. If this describes your situation, you definitely will want to take the test one or more times down the road.

WHEN YOU'RE READY

With that caveat, let's begin.

- **Step 1.** Go through the list of 135 statements in the questionnaire. For each one, mark to what extent the statement has been true of your life: Much, Some, Little or Not At All. **Warning!** Do not score according to what you think *should* be true of your life or what you *hope* might be true in the future. Be honest and score each question on the basis of actual past experience. In most cases, the answer that comes first to your mind will turn out to be the most valid answer. The more you find yourself pondering, the fuzzier your answer might be.

· **Step 2.** When you are finished, calculate your score by means of the scoring chart. Go back through your 135 answers and give yourself 3 points for Much; 2 points for Some; 1 point for Little; and 0 for Not at All. Then add up the total for each of the rows A through AA. You will immediately see which gifts are strongest and which are weakest. Compare your score with the definitions in the glossary.

· **Step 3.** Finally, to gain a preliminary evaluation of where your gifts may lie, complete the exercises in Step 3: Gifts and Ministries Analysis. Explore with friends the implications this might have for your ongoing ministry in the Body of Christ.

Reproduction of this questionnaire is prohibited.

STEP 1: WAGNER-MODIFIED HOUTS QUESTIONNAIRE

For each statement, mark to what extent it is true of your life: **M**uch, **S**ome, **L**ittle or **N**ot at All

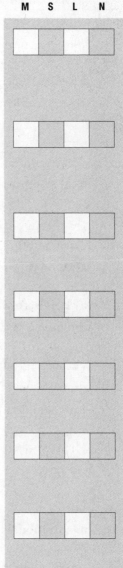

M   S   L   N

1. I have a desire to speak direct messages that I receive from God in order to edify, exhort or comfort others.

2. I have enjoyed ministering to a certain group of people over a long period of time, sharing personally in their successes and their failures.

3. People have told me that I have helped them learn biblical truths in a meaningful way.

4. I have applied spiritual truth effectively to critical situations in my own life.

5. Others have told me I have helped them to discern key and important facts of Scripture.

6. I have verbally encouraged and helped the wavering, the troubled or the discouraged.

7. Others in my church have noted that I am able to see through phoniness before it is evident to other people.

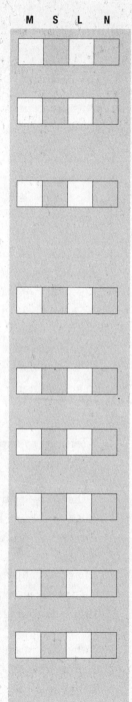

M S L N

8. I find I manage money well in order to give liberally to the Lord's work.

9. I have assisted Christian leaders to relieve them for concentrating on their essential jobs.

10. I have a desire to work with those who have physical or mental problems in order to alleviate their suffering.

11. I feel comfortable relating to people of other cultures, and they seem to accept me.

12. I have led others to a decision for salvation through faith in Christ.

13. My home is always open to people who need a place to stay.

14. When in a group, I am the one to whom others often look to for vision and direction.

15. When I speak, people seem to listen and agree.

16. When a group I am in is lacking organization, I love to step in to fill the gap.

M S L N

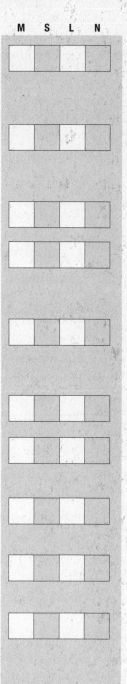

17. Others can point to specific instances in which my prayers have resulted in visible miracles.

18. In the name of the Lord, I have been used in curing diseases instantaneously.

19. I have spoken in tongues.

20. Sometimes when a person speaks in tongues, I seem to know what God is saying through them.

21. I could live more comfortably, but I choose not to in order to identify with the poor.

22. I am single and enjoy it.

23. I spend at least an hour a day in prayer.

24. I have spoken directly to evil spirits, and they have obeyed me.

25. I enjoy being called on to do odd jobs around the church.

26. A number of pastors and/or ministry leaders have told me that they desire to minister and to be held account-able under my spiritual covering.

M   S   L   N

27. I have an insatiable appetite for the presence of God.

28. Through God I have been used to reveal to others specific things that will happen in the future, and they have come to pass.

29. I have enjoyed assuming the responsibility for the spiritual well-being of a particular group of Christians.

30. I feel I can explain the New Testament teaching about the health and ministry of the Body of Christ in a relevant way.

31. I can intuitively arrive at solutions to fairly complicated problems.

32. I have had insights relating to spiritual truth that others have said helped bring them closer to God.

33. I can effectively motivate people to get busy and do what they are supposed to do.

34. I can "see" the Spirit of God resting on certain people from time to time.

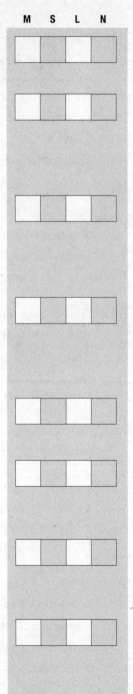

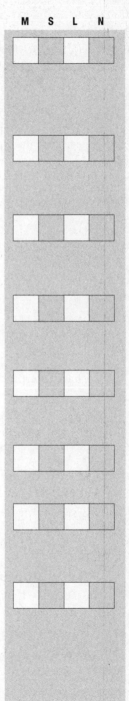

M   S   L   N

35. My giving records show that I contribute considerably more than 10 percent of my income to the Lord's work.

36. Other people have told me that I have helped them become more effective in their ministries.

37. I have offered to care for others when they have had material or physical needs.

38. I feel I could learn another language well in order to minister to those in a different culture.

39. I have shared joyfully how Christ has brought me to Himself in a way that is meaningful to nonbelievers.

40. I enjoy taking charge of church suppers or social events.

41. I have believed God for the impossible and seen it happen in a tangible way.

42. Other Christians have followed my leadership because they trusted me.

M   S   L   N

43. I enjoy handling the details of organizing ideas, people, resources and time for more effective ministry.

44. God has used me personally to perform supernatural signs and wonders.

45. I enjoy praying for sick people because I know ahead of time that many of them will be healed as a result.

46. I have spoken an immediate message of God to His people in a language I have never learned.

47. I have interpreted public tongues with the result that the Body of Christ was edified, exhorted or comforted.

48. Living a simple lifestyle is an exciting challenge for me.

49. Other people have noted that I feel more indifferent about not being married than most.

50. When I hear an urgent prayer request, I pray for that need for several days at least.

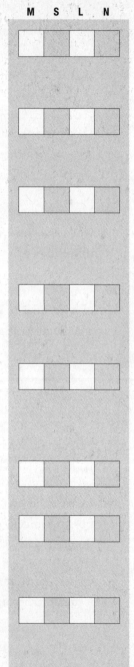

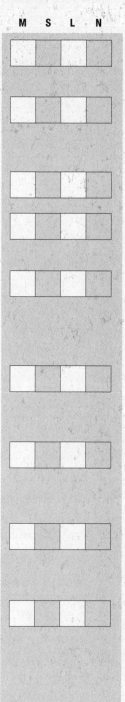

M　S　L　N

51. I have actually heard a demon speak in a loud voice.

52. I don't have many special skills, but I volunteer to do what needs to be done around the church.

53. I am known as a leader of leaders.

54. I intuitively know what should happen next in a worship service.

55. People have told me that I have communicated timely and urgent messages that must have come directly from the Lord.

56. I feel unafraid of offering spiritual guidance and direction to a group of Christians.

57. I can devote considerable time to learning new biblical truths in order to communicate them to others.

58. When other people have a problem, I can frequently guide them to the best biblical solution.

59. Through study or experience I have discerned major strategies or techniques that God seems to use in furthering His kingdom.

M   S   L   N

60. People come to me in their afflictions or suffering because they know that I will listen to them and understand.

61. I can tell with a fairly high degree of assurance when a person is afflicted by an evil spirit.

62. When I am moved by an appeal to give to God's work, I usually can find the money I need to help.

63. I have enjoyed doing routine tasks that have allowed more effective ministry on the part of others.

64. I enjoy visiting in hospitals and/or retirement homes, and feel I do well in such a ministry.

65. People of a different race or culture have been attracted to me, and we have related well.

66. Non-Christians have noted that they feel comfortable when they are around me, and that I have a positive effect on them toward developing a faith in Christ.

67. When people come to our home, they indicate that they "feel at home" with us.

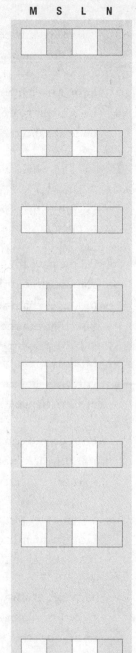

M S L N

68. Other people have told me that I had faith to accomplish what seemed impossible to them.

69. When I set goals, others seem to accept them readily.

70. I have been able to make effective and efficient plans for accomplishing the goals of a group.

71. God regularly seems to do impossible things through my life.

72. Others have told me that God healed them of an emotional problem when I ministered to them.

73. I can speak to God in a language I have never learned.

74. I have prayed that I may interpret if someone begins speaking in tongues.

75. I am not poor, but I can warmly identify with poor people.

76. I am glad I have more time to serve the Lord because I am single.

77. Day in and day out, intercessory prayer is one of my favorite ways of spending time.

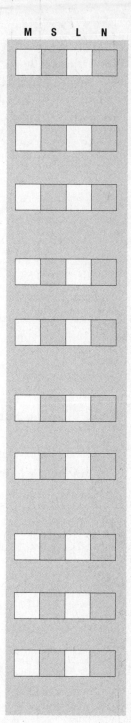

M   S   L   N

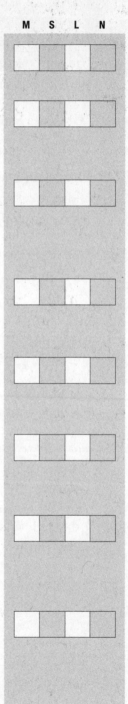

78. Others call on me when they suspect that someone is demonized.

79. Others have mentioned that I seem to enjoy routine tasks and do well at them.

80. Christian leaders seem pleased to work under my leadership, and they respect my authority when we undertake a common task.

81. During worship, I can often tell if there is a spiritual force attempting to hinder our connection with God.

82. I sometimes have a strong sense of what God wants to say to people in response to particular situations.

83. I have helped fellow believers by guiding them to relevant portions of the Bible and praying with them.

84. I feel I can communicate significant truths to others and see resulting changes in knowledge, attitudes, values or conduct.

85. Some people indicate that I have perceived and applied biblical truths to the specific needs of fellow believers.

	M	S	L	N

86. I study and read quite a bit in order to learn new biblical truths.

87. I have a desire to effectively counsel those in need.

88. I can recognize whether a person's teaching or actions are from God, from Satan, or of human origin.

89. I am so confident that God will meet my financial needs that I do not hesitate to give to His work sacrificially and consistently.

90. When I do things behind the scenes and others are helped, I am joyful.

91. People call on me to help those who are less fortunate.

92. I would be willing to leave comfortable surroundings if it would enable me to share Christ with less-fortunate people.

93. I get frustrated when others don't seem to share their faith with non-believers as much as I do.

94. Others have mentioned to me that I am a very hospitable person.

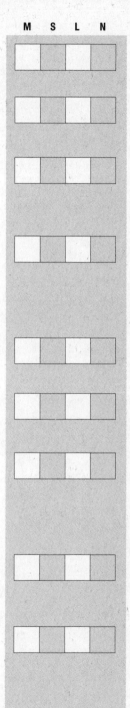

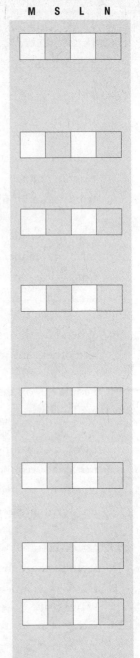

M   S   L   N

95. There have been times when I have felt sure I knew God's specific will for the future growth of His work, even when others have not been so sure.

96. When I am part of a group, others seem to back off and expect me to take leadership.

97. I am able to give directions to others without using persuasion to get them to accomplish a certain task.

98. People have told me that I was God's instrument that brought supernatural change in lives or circumstances.

99. I have prayed for others and instantaneous physical healing has often occurred.

100. When I give a public message in tongues, I expect it to be interpreted.

101. I have interpreted tongues in a way that seemed to bless others.

102. Others tell me that I sacrifice too much materially in order to fulfill God's calling.

M   S   L   N

103. I am single and have little difficulty controlling my sexual desires.

104. Others have told me that my prayers for them have been answered in tangible ways.

105. Other people have been instantly delivered from demonic oppression when I have prayed.

106. I prefer being active and doing something rather than just sitting around talking or reading or listening to a speaker.

107. I regularly receive revelation from God as to what the Holy Spirit is currently saying to the Church.

108. Others have told me that my worship helps them enter into the presence of God.

109. I frequently feel that I know exactly what God wants to do in ministry at a specific point in time.

110. People with needs have told me that I have helped them be restored to the Christian community.

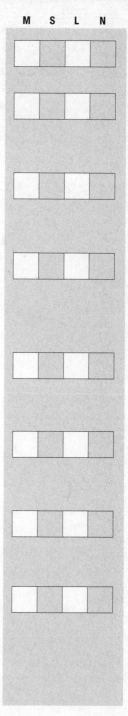

M   S   L   N

111. Studying the Bible and sharing my insights with others are very satisfying for me.

112. I have felt an unusual presence of God and personal confidence when important decisions needed to be made.

113. I have the ability to discover new truths for myself through reading or observing situations firsthand.

114. I have helped others find a biblical solution to their affliction or suffering.

115. I can tell whether a person speaking in tongues is genuine.

116. I have been willing to maintain a lower standard of living in order to benefit God's work.

117. When I serve the Lord, I truthfully don't care if someone else gets the credit for what I do.

118. I frequently enjoy spending time with a lonely, shut-in person or with someone in prison.

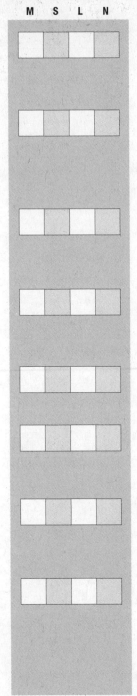

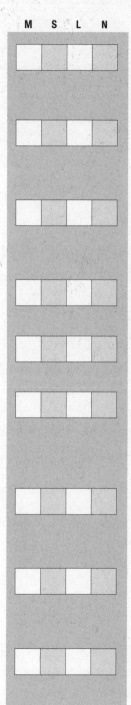

	M	S	L	N

119. More than most, I have had a strong desire to see peoples of other countries won to the Lord.

120. I am attracted to nonbelievers mainly because of my desire to win them to Christ.

121. I have desired to make my home available to those in the Lord's service whenever needed.

122. Others have told me that I am a person of unusual vision, and I agree.

123. When I am in charge, things seem to run smoothly.

124. I have enjoyed bearing the responsibility for the success of a particular task within my church or in the workplace.

125. In the name of the Lord, I have been able to help blind people receive their sight.

126. When I pray for the sick, either I or they feel sensations of tingling or warmth.

127. When I speak in tongues to a group, I believe it is edifying to the Lord's Body.

M S L N

128. I have interpreted tongues in such a way that the message appeared to be directly from God.

129. Poor people accept me easily because I choose to live on their level.

130. I readily identify with Paul's desire for others to be single as he was.

131. When I pray, God frequently speaks to me, and I recognize His voice.

132. I regularly cast out demons in Jesus' name.

133. I respond cheerfully when asked to do a job, even if it seems menial.

134. When I call Christian leaders to come together for a certain purpose, a significant number of them respond.

135. I have a compelling desire to lead others into an experience with God.

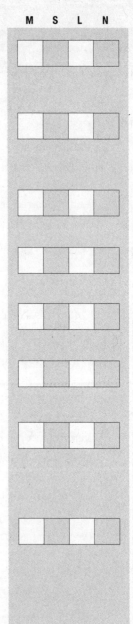

STEP 2: WAGNER-MODIFIED HOUTS CHART

In the grid below, enter the numerical value of each of your responses next to the number of the corresponding statement from *step 1*.

Much = 3   Some = 2   Little = 1   Not at All = 0

Then add up the five numbers that you have recorded in each row and place the sum in the "Total" column.

		Statement						Total	Gift
A	1		28		55		82		109		Prophecy
B	2		29		56		83		110		Pastor
C	3		30		57		84		111		Teaching
D	4		31		58		85		112		Wisdom
E	5		32		59		86		113		Knowledge
F	6		33		60		87		114		Exhortation
G	7		34		61		88		115		Discerning of Spirits
H	8		35		62		89		116		Giving
I	9		36		63		90		117		Helps
J	10		37		64		91		118		Mercy
K	11		38		65		92		119		Missionary
L	12		39		66		93		120		Evangelist
M	13		40		67		94		121		Hospitality
N	14		41		68		95		122		Faith
O	15		42		69		96		123		Leadership
P	16		43		70		97		124		Administration
Q	17		44		71		98		125		Miracles
R	18		45		72		99		126		Healing
S	19		46		73		100		127		Tongues
T	20		47		74		101		128		Interpret. of Tongues
U	21		48		75		102		129		Voluntary Poverty
V	22		49		76		103		130		Celibacy
W	23		50		77		104		131		Intercession
X	24		51		78		105		132		Deliverance
Y	25		52		79		106		133		Service
Z	26		53		80		107		134		Apostle
AA	27		54		81		108		135		Leading Worship

STEP 3: GIFTS AND MINISTRIES ANALYSIS

1. Using the results of the scoring chart in *step 2*, enter below in the "Dominant" section your three highest-rated gifts. Then enter in the "Subordinate" section the next three highest-scoring gifts. In case of some ties, do not hesitate to add lines to the "Dominant" section. This will give you a *tentative* evaluation of where your gifts may lie.

Dominant: 1. _____

                    2. _____

                    3. _____

Subordinate: 1. _____

                    2. _____

                    3. _____

2. What ministries are you *now* performing (formally or informally) in the Body?

_____

_____

_____

_____

_____

_____

_____

_____

_____

_____

3. Are there any of these ministries that you are not especially gifted for? If so, God may be calling you to consider changes.

_____

_____

_____

_____

_____

_____

_____

_____

_____

4. Is your vocational status lay or clergy?

_____

5. In light of your gift cluster and vocational status, what are some ministry models or roles suitable for you? What specific roles in the Body of Christ, including the workplace, has God possibly gifted you for?

_____

_____

_____

_____

_____

_____

_____

_____

_____

6. Discuss your findings with other believers who know you in order to evaluate your conclusions. Record their comments in the space provided.

_____

_____

_____

_____

_____

_____

_____

_____

THE NEXT STEP

Now that you have begun to discover which gifts the Holy Spirit has given you and which gifts He has not given you, you may be asking yourself, *What is the next step?* I suggest that you reread chapter 6 and choose another suggestion that I offer there.

For example, you may want to begin by studying the various gifts that the spiritual-gifts questionnaire indicated you have. Look in a concordance to find Scriptures that talk about these gifts and about Biblical characters who possessed them. Ask present-day people who possess these gifts to teach you more about them, or read a book by people who are knowledge-able about them.

You may also want to begin practicing these gifts in your local church or another ministry. If you feel that you might have the gift of teaching, try teaching Sunday School to children, youth or adults. If the gift of administration, offer to serve in your church's office or to coordinate an upcoming event. If the gift of missionary, take a short-term mission trip with your church or a mission organization.

Please consult the counsel of those who know you best—your family, your pastor, your friends and yourself. Ask them which gifts they have seen you use that have had an impact on their lives or others' lives. Don't forget to ask yourself which gifts you enjoy using.

This is your opportunity to dream with God! As you use the gifts that He has given you, He may lead you to use them in a different way than is presently occurring in your city or the world. Perhaps God will drop the desire into your heart to use your gift of worship leading to bring freedom to inmates in a nearby prison or your gift of mercy to comfort victims of catastrophes around the world.

What a privilege it is to dream God's dreams! Not only do you get to experience the joy of effectively touching people's lives, but you also get to contribute to the Body of Christ's functioning as God designed it to. And most important, our heavenly Father and His Son will be glorified.

Study Guide

CHAPTER 1
A FAST TRACK FOR DISCOVERING YOUR SPIRITUAL GIFTS

Introduction

Although teaching on spiritual gifts is prominent in the New Testament, it is not often taught in churches today. Why do you think this is the case?

_____

_____

_____

_____

Read 1 Corinthians 12:1-11. What are some of the gifts that Paul lists in this passage?

_____

_____

_____

_____

What interests you about these verses? Do you have any of the gifts listed here? If so, which ones? How do you know?

_____

_____

_____

_____

Rediscovering Our Spiritual Gifts

The 1970s brought widespread interest in moving beyond creeds and theologies with regard to the Holy Spirit. Why do you think this movement ignited at that particular time? What were people looking for?

_____

_____

_____

One facet of this new experience with the Holy Spirit was the rediscovery of spiritual gifts. What does the word "rediscovery" signify? What are some examples of this type of rediscovery in your own life even if you are born after the 1970s?

_____

_____

_____

How would you describe your relationship with the Holy Spirit?

_____

_____

_____

Fixing the Date

During the birth of the classical Pentecostal movement in the early 1900s, Pentecostal leaders wanted to influence major Christian denominations from within but found their movement incompatible with mainline American churches. Why do you think this was the case?

_____

_____

_____

Have you resisted new ideas in your own life? If so, what caused you to resist them?

_____

_____

_____

_____

Read Acts 9:1-9. What happened to Paul in this passage? How did that forever transform his life? How did his transformation affect the Church?

_____

_____

_____

_____

"Through their discovery of how the gifts of the Spirit were intended to operate in the Body of Christ, the Holy Spirit is now being transformed from abstract doctrine to dynamic experience across the board" (page 9). What are some examples of dynamic transformation in your life? In the lives of people you know?

_____

_____

_____

_____

Witnessing the Demise of Cessationism

For years, "cessationism"—the view that the more spectacular spiritual gifts ceased with the apostles—has been a prevailing doctrine in the Church. Why have some churches adopted this viewpoint? Why don't we often see the same types of miracles today as in the Early Church?

_____

_____

_____

_____

Are you inclined to hold the view of cessationism? Why or why not?

_____

_____

_____

_____

Realizing the Ministry of All Believers

According to 1 Peter 4:10, how are we to use the spiritual gifts we have been given? How is this action an extension of God's grace to others?

_____

_____

_____

What concerns do you have about spiritual gifts?

_____

_____

_____

_____

Review the discussion about the priesthood of all believers and the ministry of all believers on page 11. In your opinion, what is the difference between the two?

_____

_____

_____

_____

_____

Spiritual gifts are given for ministry. What are ways you have or will use your gifts, whether or not you have discovered all that you may possess?

_____

_____

_____

_____

_____

In John 14:12, Jesus told His disciples (and us) that they would do even greater works than He did on earth. What do you think Jesus meant by this? How could we do greater works than Jesus Himself? How does this relate to the use of spiritual gifts?

_____

_____

_____

_____

_____

CHAPTER 2
BEING EVERYTHING THAT GOD WANTS YOU TO BE

Introduction

What do you remember about your early walk with Christ? How have you learned to more fully live the Christian life?

_____

_____

_____

_____

Read Romans 12:3-6. What are some conclusions that you could draw from the phrase "God has dealt to each one a measure of faith" (v. 3)?

_____

_____

_____

_____

What Is the Body of Christ?

What does the term "Body of Christ" mean to you? How does this phrase help you picture God's plan for His Church?

_____

_____

_____

_____

Read Romans 12:2. What is one essential step toward doing the "good and effective and perfect will of God"?

_____

_____

_____

_____

Who Has Spiritual Gifts?

What has been your personal experience with spiritual gifts up to this point in your life?

_____

_____

_____

_____

Read 1 Corinthians 12:7-10. In your opinion, what should the Church look like under the manifestation of the Spirit as mentioned in this passage?

_____

_____

_____

_____

What Are Gift-Mixes?

What is meant by the term "gift-mixes"?

_____

_____

_____

_____

Describe the gift-mix you see in a sibling or a close friend. How have you seen that person use his or her gift-mix?

_____

_____

_____

_____

What motivates you to discover, develop and use your own spiritual gift-mix?

_____

_____

_____

_____

What Is the Relationship Between God's Gifts and God's Call?

How have you responded to God's general call on your life? In what ways have you struggled?

_____

_____

_____

_____

Read 2 Timothy 3:16. Describe a time when God equipped you to better serve him. What happened?

_____

_____

_____

_____

What Is a Spiritual Gift?

"A spiritual gift is a special attribute given by the Holy Spirit to every member of the Body of Christ, according to God's grace, for use within the context of the Body" (page 19). Which of the elements within this definition hold special meaning for you? Explain why.

_____

_____

_____

_____

_____

We often desire first and receive second. What was a time in your spiritual life when the opposite was true?

_____

_____

_____

_____

When have you felt like the "Lone Ranger" in ministry? What worked and what didn't work about this situation?

_____

_____

_____

_____

How have you brought ministry into the workplace? What are the advantages of engaging in "faith at work" during the week?

_____

_____

_____

_____

Are You Ready to Discover, Develop and Use Your Gift?

Keeping in mind other worthy spiritual exercises such as worship and prayer, how do you rate the importance of discovering, developing and using your spiritual gifts? What is your reasoning?

_____

_____

_____

_____

Have you ever known someone who squandered his or her spiritual gift? Why do you think God placed that gift in that person?

_____

_____

_____

_____

What Are the Benefits of Spiritual Gifts?

Think about a person you know who has demonstrated thoughtful use of his or her spiritual gifts. How has that person inspired you to use your own gifts?

_____

_____

_____

Describe a time when it was difficult to follow a particular call on your life to use your gift. How did God help you through this time?

_____

_____

_____

_____

_____

How does knowing about spiritual gifts help the Church as a whole?

_____

_____

_____

_____

_____

CHAPTER 3
HOW MANY GIFTS ARE THERE?

Introduction

Think about a time when you played sports or served with a group of people in ministry. In what ways was your team successful? In what ways did your team fall short?

_____

_____

_____

_____

What are three characteristics of a healthy team?

_____

_____

_____

_____

_____

Outlining the Three Key Lists

In Romans 12:6-8, Paul writes, "Having then gifts differing according to the grace that is given to us, let us use them." What is your understanding of grace? How do you think grace is related to spiritual gifts?

_____

_____

_____

_____

Read 1 Corinthians 12:28. Do you believe there is a ranking among some spiritual gifts? Why or why not?

_____

_____

_____

_____

In Ephesians 4:3, Paul writes that believers should endeavor "to keep the unity of the Spirit in the bond of peace." Describe a time in ministry when you experienced disunity. Did that experience hinder your faith in God? Why do you think it did or did not?

_____

_____

_____

_____

Which, if any, of the gifts listed in this section have you never heard of before? Which of these gifts stand out to you as perhaps being one or more of your own?

_____

_____

_____

_____

Completing the Master List

Are there any gifts on this master list on pages 27-29 that you found surprising? Why or why not?

_____

_____

_____

_____

Determining Whether All Gifts Are Mentioned in the Bible

In your opinion, why might God give gifts to certain believers that are not specifically mentioned in the Bible?

_____

_____

_____

_____

After reviewing my list of 28 spiritual gifts, do you believe any are missing? If so, what are they?

_____

_____

_____

_____

Distinguishing Gifts from Offices

Think of a time when you took a job or volunteer position that you felt unqualified to handle. Whether or not the situation improved, what did you learn from the experience?

_____

_____

_____

_____

If you believe you have received a gift from God, but have not fully embraced it, what has kept you from displaying the fruit of that gift?

_____

_____

_____

_____

Recognizing that Every Gift Is in the Minority

Think about your circle of friends. What specific gifts are evident among them? How has the gift-mix helped or hurt your group to be unified?

_____

_____

_____

_____

_____

Have you ever prayed for a gift that you never received? If so, how did you reconcile this with your faith?

_____

_____

_____

_____

Pairing Up: Hyphenated Gifts

What is a "hyphenated" gift?

_____

_____

_____

If you could affirm that you possess any hyphenated gifts, how would that affect the way you used them?

_____

_____

_____

_____

When have you felt "frozen" in regard to your gifts? What part does fear play in your ability to fully embrace your gifts?

_____

_____

_____

_____

_____

_____

Honoring All Variations and Degrees of Gifts

Look over the master list of 28 gifts and choose one. In what ways have you witnessed that particular gift being manifested?

_____

_____

_____

_____

_____

Read Matthew 25:14-30, the Parable of the Talents. What do you think Jesus meant when He said that the man in the story gave "to each according to his own ability" (v. 15)? How do you think this could relate to spiritual gifts?

_____

_____

_____

_____

Classifying the Gifts

Prior to reading this chapter, in what ways have you seen spiritual gifts classified?

_____

_____

_____

_____

_____

Do you prefer classifying gifts or using an open-ended approach? Explain.

_____

_____

_____

_____

_____

CHAPTER 4
FOUR DANGER SIGNS TO AVOID

Introduction

Has there been a time in your faith walk when you changed your mind wholeheartedly about something you once believed? If so, how did your change of mind come about?

_____

_____

_____

_____

_____

George Barna's Wake-up Call

Do you believe that God has given you a spiritual gift? Why or why not?

_____

_____

_____

_____

_____

How have you begun to rethink the topic of spiritual gifts?

_____

_____

_____

_____

_____

The State of the Church

Between 1995 and 2000, churches belonging to what I call the New Apostolic Reformation grew swiftly, but their teachings on spiritual gifts and their practice of them were weak. Why do you think this was the case?

_____

_____

_____

_____

_____

There are many urban legends that are prevalent today, such as the claim that chewing gum takes seven years for the body to digest or the idea that eating less than an hour before swimming will cause cramps. Why do you think misperceptions such as these persist?

_____

_____

_____

_____

_____

"Classical Pentecostalism teaches that there are nine gifts of the Holy Spirit, all found in the first part of 1 Corinthians 12" (see page 40). Have you ever believed this theory? If so, how have you been challenged by the contents of this book so far?

_____

_____

_____

_____

_____

Have you ever been surprised by a spiritual gift you have received? If so, how?

_____

_____

_____

_____

Do you believe that spiritual gifts are directly connected to the strength of your faith? Why or why not?

_____

_____

_____

_____

_____

Spiritual Gifts: Lifetime Possessions

"Once a person is given a bona fide spiritual gift, it is a lifetime possession" (page 42). What Scriptural evidence supports this claim?

_____

_____

_____

_____

_____

Has there been a time in your life when you felt your gift waning? If so, why do you think that was the case?

_____

_____

_____

_____

How can you refresh a spiritual gift that has been given to you?

_____

_____

_____

Dominant and Subordinate Gifts

Why do some gifts in believers become dominant over time? What is the danger in allowing a gift to become dormant?

_____

_____

_____

_____

How have you been stretched in the area of your spiritual gifts? How has the ranking order of your gifts, as you understand it, affected your spiritual growth?

_____

_____

_____

_____

Abuse of Spiritual Gifts

Of the two pitfalls mentioned earlier in this chapter—a short list of gifts and the situational view of spiritual gifts—which has had the greatest impact on you? Why?

_____

_____

_____

_____

Read 1 Corinthians 12:1-13. What did Paul mean in verse 1 when he wrote, "Concerning spiritual gifts, brethren, I do not want you to be ignorant"? What does Paul say in verse 12 about how we as the Church should function in our gifts?

_____

_____

_____

_____

_____

Do you believe that all spiritual gifts are created equal? Why or why not? Ponder this for a moment. Why might someone take the opposite view?

_____

_____

_____

_____

_____

Now that you know more about what the Bible teaches about spiritual gifts, how do you think your reactions will change toward those individuals who have accomplished extraordinary things during their lifetimes?

_____

_____

_____

_____

_____

CHAPTER 5
CLEARING AWAY THE CONFUSION

Don't Confuse Spiritual Gifts with Natural Talents

Read Genesis 1:26-27. What does being created in the image of God mean to you?

_____

_____

_____

_____

_____

How would you describe the difference between a natural talent and a spiritual gift? Why do you think God created natural talents apart from spiritual gifts?

_____

_____

_____

_____

As noted on page 20, charisma is the common Greek word for spiritual gift, and its root word, charis, means "grace." How have scholars (such as Max Weber) secularized the word charisma?

_____

_____

_____

_____

_____

What are the implications for secularizing words related to spiritual things?

_____

_____

_____

_____

"God may take an unbeliever's natural talent and transform it into a spiritual gift when that person is saved and becomes a member of the Body of Christ" (page 51). Can you name an example of this?

_____

_____

_____

_____

How have you changed since becoming a believer? What has surprised you?

_____

_____

_____

_____

Don't Confuse Spiritual Gifts with the Fruit of the Spirit

Read Galatians 5:22-23.Where do you see yourself regarding the fruit of the Spirit in your daily life?

_____

_____

_____

_____

How is the use of gifts different from the operation of the fruit of the Spirit?

_____

_____

_____

_____

Keeping in mind these differences you noted, do you think the presence of fruit of the Spirit is important when using spiritual gifts? Why or why not?

_____

_____

_____

_____

_____

What was one time when you experienced charisma in ministry without the presence of the fruit of the Spirit?

_____

_____

_____

_____

Spiritual gifts are temporal. Why do you think God created them only for life on earth? Does that make them any less important in your mind? Explain.

_____

_____

_____

_____

If God did not intend for the fruit of the Spirit and spiritual gifts to be confused, why do you think they are often mentioned in tandem in the Bible?

_____

_____

_____

_____

_____

_____

Don't Confuse Spiritual Gifts with Christian Roles

Faith is crucial to the life of every believer; however, the gift of faith is given only to some. How might everyday faith look the same as the gift of faith? How might they look different?

_____

_____

_____

_____

George Müller and Bill Bright were two individuals who had the gift of faith. Who do you know that has this gift? How do they exercise it?

_____

_____

_____

_____

_____

When have you made an effort to do something that doesn't come easily to you in order to fulfill your role as a Christian? What sustained you?

_____

_____

_____

_____

What does the term "spiritually arrogant" mean to you? When have you experienced it in action?

_____

_____

_____

_____

What was a time when you did something "creative" with one of your gifts?

_____

_____

_____

_____

What are some Christian roles that you have practiced? What did you learn from them?

_____

_____

_____

What personal examples can you give for Christian roles you have fulfilled that were not one of your spiritual gifts? Describe the experience.

_____

_____

_____

_____

Don't Confuse Spiritual Gifts with Counterfeit Gifts

Read 2 Corinthians 11:12-15. What was a time in your experience when the devil's workings were exposed?

_____

_____

_____

_____

How does God help believers discern between genuine gifts and counterfeit gifts?

_____

_____

_____

_____

How are we as believers to deal with counterfeit gifts when they are exposed?

_____

_____

_____

_____

CHAPTER 6
THE FIVE STEPS FOR DISCOVERING YOUR SPIRITUAL GIFTS

Introduction

Read Matthew 16:18 and Acts 2:42-47. What are some of the activities in which the newly formed Church engaged? What are some ways that modern day churches have built on these activities?

_____

_____

_____

_____

_____

How does God speak to you? How do you know it is Him who is speaking?

_____

_____

_____

_____

Be Mindful of the Four Fundamental Prerequisites

Review the four prerequisites on pages 64-66 (be a Christian; believe in spiritual gifts; be willing to work; be prayerful). Are there any that cause you to struggle? Explain.

_____

_____

_____

_____

_____

Do you believe that God wants to help you discover and develop your spiritual gifts? Why or why not?

_____

_____

_____

_____

Step 1: Explore the Possibilities

How often do you study God's Word? Do you desire to make any adjustments to your Bible reading habits? Why or why not?

_____

_____

_____

_____

What was a time when your understanding of God's Word went from passive to active? What happened when you felt that shift?

_____

_____

_____

_____

Have you ever disagreed with your church on a matter that was fundamental to you? If so, how did you handle that disagreement? What would you do differently now? What would you do the same?

_____

_____

_____

_____

Do you think the Church needs to put out "Help Wanted" signs to guarantee that all the gifts of the Spirit will be present and active within its doors? Why or why not?

_____

_____

_____

_____

_____

Read Proverbs 11:14. Think of a time when a multitude of counselors helped you come to a better understanding or decision about a matter. How did you discern whether the input you received was truly wise?

_____

_____

_____

_____

How do gifted people around you help you to examine your own areas of giftedness?

_____

_____

_____

_____

Read 2 Corinthians 10:10-13. What do these verses teach you about the practice and discussion of your own gifts?

_____

_____

_____

_____

_____

Step 2: Experiment with as Many Gifts as You Can

Do you think it is possible to "grow" into a gift? Why or why not?

_____

_____

_____

_____

What is essential to you as you pursue growth in your particular gifts?

_____

_____

_____

_____

Name a time when you stepped out in faith to serve in your church (or other ministry) and discovered—without a doubt—that you had not discovered your spiritual gift. What happened?

_____

_____

_____

_____

_____

Would you regard that as a positive or negative experience? Why?

_____

_____

_____

_____

Step 3: Examine Your Feelings

Read Psalm 37:4. As you have delighted yourself in the Lord, how have your desires changed?

_____

_____

_____

How much weight do your feelings have when it comes to making decisions? How has this served you well? When has it been a problem?

_____

_____

_____

Step 4: Evaluate Your Effectiveness

Think of a time when your effort in ministry had an overwhelmingly positive effect. What has kept you grounded? If you struggle to stay humble in the face of these types of experiences, how are you coping?

_____

_____

_____

_____

In your opinion, what are some traps that Christians should watch out for when using their spiritual gifts?

_____

_____

_____

_____

Step 5: Expect Confirmation from the Body

Why is it critical for a gift to be confirmed by others in your church?

_____

_____

_____

_____

What is the danger in assuming you have a gift that you actually do not possess?

_____

_____

_____

_____

Find Your Spiritual Gift!

Review the letter from Pastor Joe Harding on pages 80-81. Why do you think God allows us the freedom to choose between two positive ideas?

_____

_____

_____

_____

What is one step that you are willing to take to pursue your spiritual gifts?

_____

_____

_____

_____

_____

CHAPTER 7
LET'S GET STARTED!

Before You Start

Spend a few moments in prayer before answering the Wagner-Modified Houts Questionnaire. Ask God to help you answer fully and honestly and to aid you as you use the results to discover your spiritual gifts.

When You're Ready

Follow the guidelines to complete and analyze the Wagner-Modified Houts Questionnaire.

The Next Step

What are your next steps?

_____

_____

_____

How do you plan to practice the gifts He has revealed to you? Record your plan on the lines below.

_____

_____

_____

_____

_____

_____

Glossary
of Spiritual Gifts

This glossary contains the definitions of the 28 spiritual gifts covered in this book. They are in alphabetical order for your convenience. Experience has shown that many people come with presuppositions about certain gifts, so in some cases a note of explanation has been added to the definition.

The questions on the Wagner-Modified Houts Questionnaire are premised on these definitions of the gifts.

Administration: The gift of administration is the special ability that God gives to certain members of the Body of Christ to understand clearly the immediate and long-range goals of a particular unit of the Body and to devise and execute effective plans for the accomplishment of those goals (see Luke 14:28-30; Acts 6:1-7; 27:11; 1 Cor. 12:28; Titus 1:5).

Apostle: The gift of apostle is the special ability that God gives to certain members of the Body of Christ to assume and to exercise divinely imparted authority in order to establish the foundational government of an assigned sphere of ministry within the Church. An apostle hears from the Holy Spirit and sets things in order accordingly for the Church's health, growth, maturity and outreach (see Luke 6:12-13; 1 Cor. 12:28; Eph. 2:20; 4:11-13).

Note: "Church" refers to the believers who gather weekly and also to the believers scattered in the workplace.

Celibacy: The gift of celibacy is the special ability that God gives to certain members of the Body of Christ to remain single and enjoy it and not suffer undue sexual temptations (see Matt. 19:10-12; 1 Cor. 7:7-8).

Deliverance: The gift of deliverance is the special ability that God gives to certain members of the Body of Christ to cast out demons and evil spirits (see Matt. 12:22-32; Luke 10:12-20; Acts 8:5-8; 16:16-18). *Note:* This gift has also been referred to as the gift of exorcism; however, that term has been degraded by its frequent use by those practicing occult exorcism, a counterfeit form of deliverance.

Discerning of Spirits: The gift of discerning (or discernment) of spirits is the special ability that God gives to certain members of the Body of Christ to know with assurance whether certain behaviors purported to be of God are in reality divine, human or satanic (see Matt. 16:21-23; Acts 5:1-11; 16:16-18; 1 Cor. 12:10; 1 John 4:1-6).

Evangelist: The gift of evangelist is the special ability that God gives to certain members of the Body of Christ to share the gospel with unbelievers in such a way that men and women become Jesus' disciples and responsible members of the Body of Christ (see Acts 8:5-6,26-40; 14:21; 21:8; Eph. 4:11-13; 2 Tim. 4:5).

Exhortation: The gift of exhortation—sometimes called the gift of counseling—is the special ability that God gives to certain members of the Body of Christ to minister words of comfort, consolation, encouragement and counsel to other members of the Body in such a way that they feel helped and healed (see Acts 14:22; Rom. 12:8; 1 Tim. 4:13; Heb. 10:25).

Faith: The gift of faith is the special ability that God gives to certain members of the Body of Christ to discern with extraordinary confidence the will and purposes of God for the future of His work (see Acts 11:22-24; 27:21-25; Rom. 4:18-21; 1 Cor. 12:9; Heb. 11).

Giving: The gift of giving is the special ability that God gives to certain members of the Body of Christ to contribute their material resources to the work of the Lord liberally and cheerfully, above and beyond the tithes and offerings expected of all believers (see Mark 12:41-44; Rom. 12:8; 2 Cor. 8:1-7; 9:2-8).

Healing: The gift of healing is the special ability that God gives to certain members of the Body of Christ to serve as human intermediaries through whom it pleases God to cure illness and restore health apart from the use of natural means (see Acts 3:1-10; 5:12-16; 9:32-35; 28:7-10; 1 Cor. 12:9,28).

Helps: The gift of helps is the special ability that God gives to certain members of the Body of Christ to invest the talents they have in the life and ministry of other members of the Body, thus enabling those others to increase the effectiveness of their own spiritual gifts (see Mark 15:40-41; Luke 8:2-3; Acts 9:36; Rom. 16:1-2; 1 Cor. 12:28). *Note:* The gift of helps may be confused with the gift of service. Someone with the gift of helps usually aids one individual (e.g., an administrative assistant), while a person with the gift of service is willing to do whatever is necessary for a cause or project.

Hospitality: The gift of hospitality is the special ability that God gives to certain members of the Body of Christ to provide an open house and warm welcome for those in need of food and lodging (see Acts 16:14-15; Rom. 12:9-13; 16:23; Heb. 13:1-2; 1 Pet. 4:9).

Intercession: The gift of intercession is the special ability that God gives to certain members of the Body of Christ to pray for extended periods of time on a regular basis and see frequent and specific answers to their prayers to a degree much greater than that which is expected of the average Christian (see Luke 22:41-44; Acts 12:12; Col. 1:9-12; 4:12-13; 1 Tim. 2:1-2; Jas. 5:14-16).

Interpretation of Tongues: The gift of interpretation of tongues is the special ability that God gives to certain members of the Body of Christ to make known in the vernacular the message of one who speaks in tongues (see 1 Cor. 12:10,30; 14:13-14,26-28).

Knowledge: The gift of knowledge is the special ability that God gives to certain members of the Body of Christ to discover, accumulate, analyze and clarify information and ideas that are pertinent to the growth and well-being of the Body (see Acts 5:1-11; 1 Cor. 2:14; 12:8; 2 Cor. 11:6; Col. 2:2-3).

Note: Pentecostals and charismatics often use the term "word of knowledge," which is information that God gives by revelation for a certain situation. My interpretation of the charismatic "word of knowledge" is that such a gift is in reality a subset of the gift of prophecy, not the gift of knowledge. A scholar, on the other hand, would be one who has a gift of knowledge.

Leadership: The gift of leadership is the special ability that God gives to certain members of the Body of Christ to set goals in accordance with God's purpose for the future and to communicate these goals to others in such a way that they voluntarily and harmoniously work together to accomplish those goals for the glory of God (see Luke 9:51; Acts 7:10; 15:7-11; Rom. 12:8; 1 Tim. 5:17; Heb. 13:17).

Leading Worship: The gift of leading worship is the special ability that God gives to certain members of the Body of Christ to accurately discern the heart of God for a particular public worship service, to draw others into an intimate experience of God during the worship time and to allow the Holy Spirit to change directions and emphases as the service progresses (see 1 Sam. 16:23; 1 Chron. 9:33; 2 Chron. 5:12-14; Ps. 34:3).

Martyrdom: The gift of martyrdom is the special ability that God gives to certain members of the Body of Christ to undergo suffering for the faith even to death while consistently displaying a joyous and victorious attitude that brings glory to God (see Acts 22:20; 1 Cor. 13:3; Rev. 2:13; 17:6).

Mercy: The gift of mercy is the special ability that God gives to certain members of the Body of Christ to feel genuine empathy and compassion for individuals, both Christian and non-Christian, who suffer distressing physical, mental or emotional problems, and to translate that compassion into cheerfully done deeds that reflect Christ's love and alleviate the suffering (see Matt. 20:29-34; 25:34-40; Mark 9:41; Luke 10:33-35; Acts 11:28-30; 16:33-34; Rom. 12:8).

Miracles: The gift of miracles is the special ability that God gives to certain members of the Body of Christ to serve as human intermediaries through whom it pleases God to perform powerful acts that are perceived by observers to have altered the ordinary course of nature (see Acts 9:36-42; 19:11-20; 20:7-12; Rom. 15:18-19; 1 Cor. 12:10,28; 2 Cor. 12:12).

Missionary: The gift of missionary is the special ability that God gives to certain members of the Body of Christ to minister whatever other spiritual gifts they have in a second culture (see Acts 8:4; 13:2-3; 22:21; Rom. 10:15; 1 Cor. 9:19-23; Eph. 3:6-8). *Note:* The gift of missionary should not be confused with the gift of apostle. Some apostles have the gift of missionary and do cross-cultural ministry (e.g., the apostle Paul), while other apostles do not have the missionary gift and therefore they minister monoculturally (e.g., the apostle Peter).

Pastor: The gift of pastor is the special ability that God gives to certain members of the Body of Christ to assume a long-term personal responsibility for the spiritual welfare of a group of believers (see John 10:1-18; Eph. 4:11-13; 1 Tim. 3:1-7; 1 Pet. 5:1-3). *Note:* The term "pastor" is commonly used to describe the leader of a local congregation; however, many who lead churches have dominant gifts other than pastor (e.g., leader or teacher). Those leaders who do not have the dominant gift of pastor may augment their role using volunteers or staff members.

Prophecy: The gift of prophecy is the special ability that God gives to certain members of the Body of Christ to receive and communicate an immediate message of God to His people through a divinely anointed utterance (see Luke 7:26; Acts 15:32; 21:9-11; Rom. 12:6; 1 Cor. 12:10,28; Eph. 4:11-13).

Service: The gift of service—sometimes called the gift of volunteer—is the special ability that God gives to certain members of the Body of Christ to identify the unmet needs involved in a task related to God's work, and to make use of available resources to meet those needs and help accomplish the desired goals (see Acts 6:1-7; Rom. 12:7; Gal. 6:2,10; 2 Tim. 1:16-18; Titus 3:14).

Note: The gift of service may be confused with the gift of helps. See note on helps for clarification.

Teaching: The gift of teaching is the special ability that God gives to certain members of the Body of Christ to communicate information relevant to the health and ministry of the Body and its members in such a way that others will learn (see Acts 18:24-28; 20:20-21; Rom. 12:7; 1 Cor. 12:28; Eph. 4:11-13).

Tongues: The gift of tongues is the special ability that God gives to certain members of the Body of Christ (1) to speak to God in a language they have never learned and/or (2) to receive and communicate an immediate message from God to His people through a divinely anointed utterance in a language they have never learned (see Mark 16:17; Acts 2:1-13; 10:44-46; 19:1-7; 1 Cor. 12:10,28; 14:13-19).

Voluntary Poverty: The gift of voluntary poverty is the special ability that God gives to certain members of the Body of Christ to renounce material comfort and luxury and adopt a personal lifestyle equivalent to those living at the poverty level in a given society in order to serve God more effectively (see Acts 2:44-45; 4:34-37; 1 Cor. 13:1-3; 2 Cor. 6:10; 8:9).

Wisdom: The gift of wisdom is the special ability that God gives to certain members of the Body of Christ to know the mind of the Holy Spirit in such a way as to receive insight into how given knowledge may best be applied to specific needs arising in the Body of Christ (see Acts 6:3,10; 1 Cor. 2:1-13; 12:8; Jas. 1:5-6; 2 Pet. 3:15-16). *Note:* Pentecostals and charismatics often use the term "word of wisdom," meaning a revelatory message God gives to bring resolution to a certain situation. I feel the charismatic "word of wisdom" is really a subset of the gift of prophecy, not the gift of wisdom. A judge, on the other hand, would be one who has a gift of wisdom.

Discover How to Use Your
Spiritual Gifts!

Finding Your Spiritual Gifts

The easy-to-use, self-guided questionnaire that helps you identify and understand your unique God-given spiritual gifts

ISBN 978.08307.6216.3
ISBN 08307.6216.7

Your Spiritual Gifts
Can Help Your Church Grow

The bestselling guide for discovering and understanding your unique spiritual gifts and using them to bless others

ISBN 978.08307.6229.3
ISBN 08307.6229.9

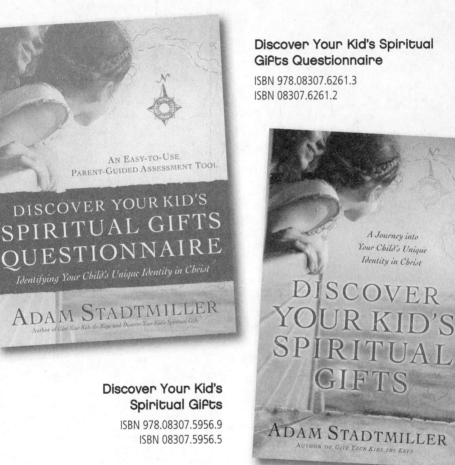